The EVERYDAY LIFE series is one of the best known and most respected of all historical works, giving detailed insight into the background life of a particular period. This edition provides an invaluable picture of prehistoric life from the New Stone Age to the Early Iron Age.

The Times Literary Supplement has commended EVERYDAY LIFE IN PREHISTORIC TIMES for its 'vivid narrative, admirably illustrated', and this new, revised edition is an outstanding account of how ordinary people lived before the historians left a written record of the past.

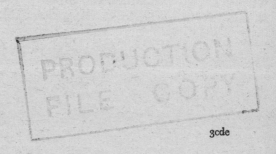

3cde

Also available in this series

**EVERYDAY LIFE
IN PREHISTORIC TIMES –
THE OLD STONE AGE**

MARJORIE AND C. H. B. QUENNELL

EVERYDAY LIFE IN PREHISTORIC TIMES – THE NEW STONE AGE

Carousel Editor: Anne Wood

TRANSWORLD PUBLISHERS LTD
A National General Company

EVERYDAY LIFE IN PREHISTORIC TIMES –
THE NEW STONE AGE

A CAROUSEL BOOK 0 552 54006 4

Originally published in Great Britain
by B. T. Batsford Ltd.

PRINTING HISTORY
Batsford edition (one volume entitled *Everyday Life in
Prehistoric Times*, which forms the Carousel edition of
Everyday Life in Prehistoric Times – The New Stone Age
and the companion Carousel volume *Everyday Life in
Prehistoric Times – The Old Stone Age*) published 1959
Fifth impression 1968
Carousel edition published 1971

Carousel Books are published by Transworld
Publishers Ltd.,
Cavendish House, 57–59 Uxbridge Road,
Ealing, London, W.5.

Made and printed in Great Britain by
Cox & Wyman Ltd., London, Reading and Fakenham

'The operations of the mind no doubt find their noblest expression in the language of speech, yet they are also eloquent in the achievements of the hand. The works of man's hands are his embodied thought, they endure after his bodily framework has passed into decay, and thus throw a welcome light on the earliest stages of his unwritten history.'

From *Ancient Hunters* by Prof. W. J. Sollas

PREFACE

THIS BOOK has come into being as a result of another that we wrote and illustrated. It was intended for boys and girls, and we called it a *History of Everyday Things in England*. An attempt was made to draw the eyes of our readers away from the Destruction which was to the fore in those days, and to present instead a picture of all the care and trouble which had gone to the Construction of the everyday things that were being destroyed. We gave the matter very careful consideration, and it seemed to us essential that the things illustrated should be of a type with which our readers would be familiar. Boys and girls, in their summer holidays, might have seen the Norman work at Norwich or Castle Rising, or the Renaissance work of Inigo Jones at Raynham. With some reluctance we made no mention of any earlier work. The doings of Roman, Saxon, and Dane were only hinted at, and the prehistoric period was not mentioned at all. We started with William the Conqueror, and finished at the start of the twentieth century.

Since we appear to have interested many boy and girl readers, we now want to fill in the long space before 1066. One is so apt to lump together all the earlier work, and think of it as having been done in a few centuries; the sense of perspective is lost. History is rather like travelling on the railway, the events flash past like telegraph posts, the nearer ones having their due spaces in between; but if we look back, the events, like the posts, are all bunched together and we cannot realize the spaces.

These spaces are as important as the events of History, and represent the periods when people were making up their minds; recovering perhaps from great disasters, or gathering their forces to go forward.

The races of mankind, like their works, develop by growth to flower and decay, but always there is a re-birth or renaissance. The Madeleine Art we illustrate died out in 12,000 B.C., yet still lives to inspire us; that is the boys and girls who want to do work, because if History is divided into events, and spaces, then the people are divided into those who have ideas, and want to do and make things, and the others who only deal in the ideas, and benefit by them.

Personally we hold that History is not just dates, but a long tale of man's life, labour and achievement; and if this be so, we cannot afford to neglect the doings of prehistoric men, who with flint for their material, made all the implements and weapons they needed for their everyday life.

We call the pick-and-shovel historian an Archaeologist, from the Greek *archaios*, ancient, and *logos*, discourse. The archaeologist is helped by the astronomers and mathematicians, who are called in to decide in matters of climatic change like the Glacial Periods. A skull is found, like the one at Swanscombe in Kent, and the anatomists examine it carefully to fit it into its place as a link in the chain of man's development. The science of man and mankind is called Anthropology, from *anthropos*, a man, and *logos*, discourse. The science of life is Biology. One must also know something of geology, which is the science that deals with the structure of the earth.

Many books have been written on Prehistoric Archaeology but these are on the whole not suitable for boys and girls. We have therefore taken the ascertained and proved facts, and have plotted these out as a plan. If our readers are interested in this plan they can themselves raise a superstructure of more advanced knowledge. We do not lay claim to any great store of archaeological knowledge ourselves, and have approached our task rather as illustrators. As painter and architect, who have been making things ourselves all our lives, we may perhaps be able to treat the work of prehistoric man in a sympathetic fashion, and hope our pictures will help boys and girls to *see* these old people a little.

This brings up the question of how we are to approach prehistoric man. We must free our minds of prejudice. Some people will say that he was a loathsome creature, incredibly dirty and unpleasant. There will be other people who will regard our friend as the Noble Savage, and clothe him in their minds with all the simple virtues. It will not do to jump to conclusions. Shall we judge him by his *work*? If we try to find out how he lived, the tools he used, and the things that he made with them, then in the end we shall have a picture in our own minds. This is the essential part of reading a book, that it should help us to form our own conclusions. So we do not seek to teach, nor do we wish to preach, but we do want to interest our readers, and here we give you fair warning. If we can do so: if this subtle little microbe can work its way into your system, and you want to find out how things were made and done, then you may become archaeologists yourselves.

MARJORIE AND C. H. B. QUENNELL

CONTENTS

ACKNOWLEDGMENTS

The Authors and Publishers wish to acknowledge the sources of the new line illustrations which are included in this edition:

Fig. 7 from *Jungsteinzeitseidlungen in Federseemoor* by R. R. Schmidt; fig. 9 from V. G. Childe in *Proc. Preh. Soc.* 1949, 77; figs. 10 and 11 after Vassits in *Prehis. Zeit.* 1910; fig. 28 from *Woodhenge* by M. and E. Cunnington (Devizes Museum publication); fig. 39 from *Urgeschichte der Bildenden Kunst in Europa* by H. Hoernes; fig. 42 from *Manuel de L'Archeologie Préhistorique* by J. Dechelette; fig. 43 from *Le Char et le traneau* by H. Breuil; fig. 46 from *A Guide to the Prehistoric Rock Engravings* by C. Bicknell; figs. 50–52 after W. J. Hemp; figs. 58, 70 and 73 from *Prehistoric Europe* by J. G. D. Clark (Methuen and Co. Ltd., 1950).

LIST OF ILLUSTRATIONS

BIBLIOGRAPHY

GENERAL PREHISTORY

Childe, V. G., *What Happened in History* (Penguin Books, 1942).

Childe, V. G., *Man Makes Himself* (Oxford, 1956).

Clark, Grahame, *Archaeology and Society* (Methuen, 1956).

Clark, Grahame, *An Outline of World Prehistory* (Cambridge, 1961).

Coon, C. P., *The Races of Europe* (Macmillan, 1939).

Davies, G. E., *The Megalith Builders of Western Europe* (Hutchinson, 1958).

LATER PREHISTORIC TIMES IN BRITAIN

Atkinson, R. J. C., *Stonehenge* (Hamilton, 1956, Penguin Books, 1960).

Bruce-Nutford, R., *Recent Archaeological Excavations in Britain* (Routledge, 1954).

Bulleid, A., *The Lake Villages of Somerset*.

Childe, V. G., *The Prehistory of Scotland* (Cambridge, 1935).

Clark, Grahame, *Prehistoric England* (Batsford, 1940).

Clarke, R. Rainbird, *East Anglia* (Thames & Hudson 1959).

Fox, Sir Cyril, *The Personality of Britain* (Cardiff, National Museum of Wales, 1959).

Fox, Sir Cyril, *A Find of the Early Iron Age from Llyn Cerrig* (Cardiff, National Museum of Wales).

Fox, Sir Cyril, *Life and Death in the Bronze Age* (Routledge, 1959).

Bibliography

Grimes, W. F., *The Prehistory of Wales* (Cardiff, National Museum of Wales, 1951).

Hawkes, Jacquetta, *Early Britain* (Collins, 1944).

Hawkes, Jacquetta and Christopher, *Prehistoric Britain* (Chatto, 1947, Penguin Books, 1949).

Piggott, Stuart, *Britain in Prehistory* (Oxford, 1949).

Piggott, Stuart, *Scotland Before History*.

O'Riordan, Sean, *Antiquities of the Irish Countryside* (Methuen, 1953).

Raftery, Joseph, *Prehistoric Ireland* (Batsford, 1951).

Stone, J. F. S., *Wessex Before the Celts* (Thames & Hudson, 1958).

GUIDE BOOKS

Hawkes, J. J., *A Guide to the Prehistoric and Roman Monuments in Britain and Wales* (Chatto, 1951).

Sieveking, Ann & G. de G., *A Short Guide to Caves of France and Northern Spain* (Vista Books, 1961).

Thomas, Nicholas, *A Guide to Prehistoric England* (Batsford, 1960).

THE NEW STONE AGE

THE New Stone Age or the Neolithic Period is recognized as the period when the first farmers arrived in England. They came on a long journey travelling very slowly for hundreds of years from the countries in the Near East where farming was first invented.

When the first Neolithic men arrived here, they would have found excellent pasture then, as now, on the Downs, and flint for their tools. They would move along the line of the old road later called the Pilgrims' Way, on the escarpment of the North Downs, secure from wolf or man. We find today traces of Neolithic man on this road; there is Kitscoty to the north-west of Maidstone; the Coldrum monument to the west on the other side of the Medway; the pit-dwellings in Rose Wood near Ightham – all dating from the New Stone Age. Neolithic man introduced sheep, goats, pigs, and cattle (*Bos longifrons*), like the small black Welsh cattle. These necessitated enclosures; so we find along the trackways on the Downs and on Salisbury Plain earthworks where cattle could be herded together for safe keeping or for slaughter.

These camps are only found in the South of England; for not only was pasture better on the Downs, but there were fewer trees. The country was far more wooded than it is now, and man had not as yet the implements with which to make extensive clearings in

Fig. 1 Dug-out canoe

the forests. It is a mistake, however, to think of these as dense tropical jungles, because the climate then was temperate, as it is now. The undrained country would have been a more formidable obstacle than the forests, and places like the Sussex Weald which was all sticky clay. The forests were full of wild animals; there was the Irish elk and the wild ox (aurochs), bears and beavers, wild cats and red deer, wild boars and the wolf, and Neolithic man hunted these with dogs.

Later and more adventurous immigrants seem to have coasted round until they came to the chalk at Eastbourne. They would have set out in their dug-out canoes (Fig. 1), and some of these have been found as long as 50 feet. On the South Downs again are earthworks and tumuli, linked up by trackways leading to Stonehenge. Others came in at the Wash, which in those days extended inland much farther than it does today, and here Icknield Way goes south to the Goring Gap on the Thames, and then by way of the Berkshire Downs again to Stonehenge. Later on Maiden Castle, near Dorchester, and its connection with the trackways, points to traffic and trade by sea.

The range of Neolithic man seems to have been the Downs, the Blackdown Hills to Devon and Cornwall, the Mendips, the Cotswolds to the Northampton Heights, the South Pennines and Lincolnshire Hills, the Yorkshire Wolds and Moors, and the Glamorgan Hills, and the north and west of Scotland, and all these parts are connected by trackways which converge on Salisbury Plain and Stonehenge, which appears to have been the richest part of England in the Neolithic and Bronze Ages, and the seat of such spiritual and civil government as there was.

It should be noted that the trackways follow the watersheds, and so avoid the crossing of rivers – a serious obstacle to flocks and herds. In later days the great river valleys formed avenues of approach for immigrants into the country, and the fact that so many of these are on the East Coast, has rendered us peculiarly liable to invasion on that side. The tide runs up the Humber and Ouse nearly to York; up the Trent to just beyond Gainsborough, and the Thames to Teddington.

Archaeologists cannot prove how many of these trackways were in use in Neolithic times, for Neolithic settlements and monuments are rare by comparison with those of the later prehistoric Ages. For the Bronze Age we have a great many of these monuments, and these can plainly be seen, especially in the south of England, strung out along the trackways, where these still exist and have not been destroyed by later ploughing – for example, on the Downs and the Salisbury Plain. We may be certain, however, that Neolithic man used the trackways or others very like them – when he moved by land and with cattle – because in heavily forested country it always pays to choose the well-drained land when you move from place to place.

In the earliest period of England's settlement by agricultural peoples – by farmers and herdsmen – we should think of people moving around at two very different speeds. First there were the explorers, the discoverers of new land, and the earliest traders, or groups of farmers who still did a considerable amount of hunting. These groups travelled far and wide by the rivers and trackways, and quite fast – even by modern standards. Then there were the tribes or large families engaged in planting corn and looking after cattle – these cleared patches of forest, near where they landed on the English coast, and only moved on two or three miles at a time, every two or three years, when they had exhausted the food for their cattle, or the possibility of growing corn in their woodland clearing. These groups took hundreds of years to cover England.

Before we examine the works of Neolithic man in more detail, it will be as well to try and find out something about him and the European Races during the Neolithic, Bronze, and Early Iron Ages. We can refer to ourselves as Anglo-Saxons or Britons, and yet be very wide of the mark. Assuming that we were cruising over Great Britain in an aeroplane, we could in a few days cover the length and breadth of the land, and if we kept our eyes open when we landed, we should find very varying types in our own country.

In parts of Essex, and the South Midlands and Chilterns; on the hills to the west of the Severn in Worcestershire, Shropshire, and Herefordshire; in Romney Marsh, the Weald, and the Isle of Ely, we should find a large proportion of dark-haired people with long heads, and the explanation of this is, that as these parts were off the main lines of Saxon immigration, the old British blood has lingered on. The Saxons penetrated into the country on the line of the

Thames, and this element is strong in Berkshire, Oxfordshire, Hampshire, Sussex, and up the Thames Valley to the Cotswolds; here you will find fair people with blue eyes. In Leicestershire and Lincolnshire are Danish types with long faces, and heads rather high behind; high cheek-bones, and well-formed noses; they appear to have driven the Anglians to the Derbyshire hills in olden days. In Yorkshire we find a typically English people; shrewd, vigorous, and obstinate; successful in business; hard-headed and practical, yet with a great love of music. In the Shetlands, Orkneys, Hebrides, and parts of Caithness are splendid men of Norwegian descent. In the Highlands a Gaelic stock, quick-tempered and emotional; in the Lowlands, and the eastern coast-lands, a frugal hardworking people descended from Angles, Danes, and immigrants from the east.

It is obvious, then, that our own island provides us with some very fair samples of the European races, and if we are to understand our own history, or discover where these types have come from, we must cross to the mainland.

The European Races have been divided into three large families or groups, the Nordic, Alpine, and Mediterranean, and the history of Europe is a recital of the migrations and minglings of these types. Nordic means Northern, and this type is sometimes called Teutonic; these people came from the steppe region to the north of the mountains between Europe and Asia. As the climate improved after the last Ice Age this became forest. The people were tall and strongboned, with fair hair, and blue eyes, and they were long-headed.

The Alpine people came from the mountain zone of Europe; they were thick-set, and round-headed.

The Mediterranean men came from the coast-lands of that sea; they were dark, long-headed, with oval faces and aquiline noses; of middle height, not more than 5 feet 6 inches, and the women shorter and not very robust.

The Nordic and Mediterranean types were probably descendants of the later long-headed people of the Old Stone Age, and the Alpine later arrivals from the east.

It is to the Mediterranean stock that we must look for the first of the Neolithic people in this country. It is thought that working along the coast-lands of the western part of the Mediterranean they struck up through the Carcassone Gap between the Pyrenees and the Cevennes, and thence through the west of France until they came to Brittany and Normandy, then worked along the coast until they came to where the Straits of Dover now are. Remember this was not done in a day, or many days, but was a movement lasting for hundreds of years.

The later Mediterranean people were the builders of the Megalithic monuments; the menhirs, dolmens, and chambered barrows which culminated in Stonehenge, and spread from the Eastern Mediterranean across to Western Europe and our own land. Megalithic is derived from two Greek words, *megas*, great, and *lithos*, stone, and its most distinctive contribution to the art of building was the evolution of the lintel; in this detail it was allied to Egyptian and Greek building. Stonehenge is the triumph of the lintel, and the main building that we know so well is believed to date from the earlier part of the Bronze Age.

These dolmen builders may have retreated before the round-headed Bronze Age men, who seem to have come from the Eastern Mediterranean, through Gaul to Britain. They were stalwart, dark, broad-headed

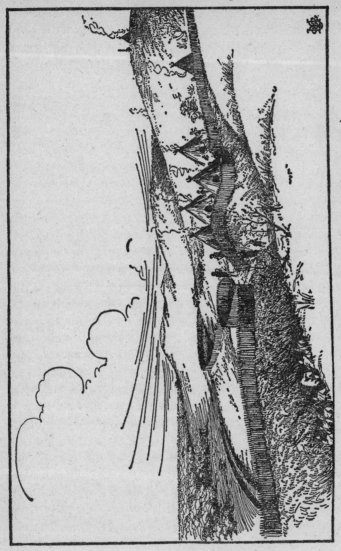

Fig. 2 Reconstruction of an Iron Age hill fort (*see page 117*)

men, and arrived here about 1800 B.C. It is thought
that these earliest round-heads were not Goidels, and
we will explain this later. It is quite possible that they
may have had something to do with megalithic building, as they associated with the Neolithic long-heads;
we know this, because in the round barrows, which are
of Bronze Age, round- and long-heads are found
buried together. The Bronze men brought with them
their flat bronze axes (Fig. 29), and if at the first they
could not manufacture these they did obtain them by
trade.

About the same time the 'Beaker' people arrived on
the north and east coasts. They are called 'Beaker'
people because of a pottery vessel found in their graves
(Fig. 48 (1)). It may not have been a drinking-cup or
beaker, but it looks like one. They may have come
from Spain or from Germany where their pottery is
equally common. These Beaker men were a mixture of
Alpine and Nordic, combining the broad heads of the
Alpine with the fair colouring, strength and length of
bone of the Nordic. They were tall and strong-
browed.

About this time we are able to find out that the
conditions of life were becoming easier. The people
lived longer lives, they were bigger than in Neolithic
times, and there was less difference between the size
of men and women.

At a later day, perhaps about 700 to 500 B.C., the
first of the Celts arrived; they were an Aryan-speaking
people who burned their dead. Here we might explain
what is meant by the Aryan-speaking peoples, because
the spread of this language is one of the wonderful
things in the world's history, like the La Madeleine
painting. The Aryan language is also described as
being Indo-European, Indo-Iranian, and Indo-Ger-

manic. Towards the end of the eighteenth century, similarities were noticed in the construction of languages seemingly so different as Sanscrit, Greek, Latin, German, and Celtic, and later all the European languages, except Turkish, Finnish, and one or two others, were added, with some modern Indian languages, to a group which has been derived from this primitive Aryan tongue. This does not mean that all the millions of Aryan-speaking people today are descended from Aryan stock; it does point to some wonderful idea which spread across Europe like a flame burning dry grass.

The exact spot where the original Aryans lived is still a matter of debate: one idea is that it was in south Russia or Hungary; another, on the Iranian plateau to the south-east of the Caspian Sea. From there the language spread south-east across the Indus into India. The route to Europe may have been to the east of the Caspian Sea and then west across the Volga, Don, and Dnieper, whence came the Beaker people. Or northwest from the Iranian plateau, and south of the Black Sea into Asia Minor and the Ægean. Now language does not spread as a fashion, but because it is the vehicle of thought embodying a dominating idea.

The diffusion of the Aryan language coincided with great changes and migrations of the European peoples. The old Neolithic civilization had carried men forward as a tribe, and in a state which did not offer much opportunity to the individual. While the pioneer work was being done, the adventurous men had plenty to occupy them, and then may have become restless as conditions became more settled, and have seized power, not necessarily from a selfish point of view, but to satisfy wider ambitions and to obtain more movement and colour in life. We come to the Age of

Heroes. The chieftain, or patriarch of the tribe, has to give way to the hero, who welds it into a nation and becomes a king.

The Celts, an Aryan-speaking, fair-haired people began to come over from the Continent about 500 B.C. bringing with them the first weapons and implements of iron. They spoke two kindred but slightly differing tongues which still persist in these islands in forms which, in the main, are not greatly altered. They were called, according to this division of speech, the Goidels and Brythons, and by Roman writers the Gauls and Britons. The descendants of the former are the Irish, the Highlanders of Scotland, and the Manx, of the latter the Welsh and the Cornish.

About 75 B.C. came the Belgae, of Celtic stock with an admixture of Germanic, and Caesar found them in the possession of south-east Britain when he arrived.

Having now given an outline sketch of the various peoples we shall meet with, we will go back to the first of these, the men of the New Stone Age. We will examine first their implements, and then later consider the work they did with these tools. These Neolithic implements are not necessarily of polished stone, as some people seem to think. Flint was still chipped as in the Old Stone Age: sometimes it was chipped and ground, or polished in parts; sometimes completely so.

At Cissbury near Worthing, and Grime's Graves near Weeting in Norfolk, the pits formed by the early miners to obtain their flints have been discovered, and it is thought the implements were roughly finished here for export. They used deer-horn picks, and shoulder-blades as shovels. These can be seen in the Prehistoric Room at the British Museum. Fig. 3 shows the miners using these deer-horn picks like you use a modern pick, but often the flint was too solid to be broken out of the chalk in this way. So the miners hammered the point of their pick into a crack in the flint and then used the long handle to lever out a flint block. The springy deer horn or antler was better than anything else could be for this purpose. If you examine these picks carefully you will see the marks where someone has hammered hard on the broadest part of the pick with a stone hammer, and lines of small holes have been found around the flint in these ancient mines. This is where someone had started to break out a piece of flint and had never come back to lever it out.

Fig. 3   Flint miners

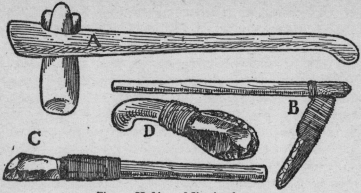

Fig. 4   Hafting of flint implements

The archaeologists who excavated at Grime's Graves in Norfolk actually found the fingerprint of a Neolithic flint miner on one of these deer-horn picks.

Fig. 4 shows a few typical implements, and the way they were hafted or had handles fitted. Fig. 4(A) is the celt, or axe, and is the Neolithic descendant of the hand-axe of the Old Stone Age. Celts have been found varying from an inch or so long up to 15 inches or 16 inches, and were the most important implements of Neolithic man. They were driven into the head of a wooden handle as at A, and then wedged from the top. Sometimes the celt was fixed into a deer-horn socket driven into the wood. With celts trees were cut down and all the rough carpentry done. The stone celt or axe was the forerunner of the bronze axe, and led to the iron axe which has been one of the most useful tools of man throughout the ages. Fig. 4(A) shows a polished stone celt. These at first were chipped out of flint. Then the cutting edge was ground, and finally the whole celt polished. Fig. 4(B) shows a rougher, unpolished type, hafted at right angles to the handle for use as an adze; this may have been used like a hoe to chop towards the foot, and must have been very useful in making dug-out canoes. Rougher stones mounted in this way were used perhaps as hoes for agriculture. For this method of hafting any branched stick could be used, and the flint bound on with raw-hide thongs. Fig. 4(C) shows how a chisel-shaped flake could be mounted, and Fig. 4(D) a scraper. Scrapers were as useful and general in the New, as in the Old Stone Age, and probably served to remove the fat from skins and to scrape wood. A very usual shape was that of an oyster-shell; the Eskimo use these, and mount them in ivory handles, and their flaying knives are like the thin oval flakes of greenstone, found in Scotland, and called Picts' knives. Fig. 5(A) shows a polished stone celt hafted at right angles for use as an adze. Fig. 5(B) is a stone axe with double edge, and Fig. 5(C) a stone hammer. In thinking of how these were made we must remember the extraordinary patience of the savage.

The Neolithic implement maker used volcanic rocks for his axes, and after roughly trimming these to shape, finished by grinding the axe on a grindstone – not one that runs round, but by rubbing the axe on a stone, as the carpenter sharpens his plane iron. The boring of the hole was done last, with a stick, or hollow bone, and sand and water. Any sand hard enough to scratch the stone would cut the hole in time. The drill could have been turned with a bow. Odysseus drills out the eye of

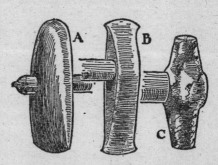

Fig. 5   Stone axes and hammers

Polyphemus by means of a stake with a leather thong around it, 'as when a man bores a ship's timber'.

Some of the stone axes have one edge and a rounded head, and may have been used for splitting wood, by hammering the head with a wooden mallet. Others have a purposely blunted edge, as if for use as battle-axes, with less chance of cutting the wielder, and just as much power to damage the enemy. Amusing traditions have gathered around the old stone celts; the country people in the past thought they were thunder-bolts. Stone hammers were known in Scotland, until the end of the eighteenth century, as Purgatory Ham-mers, and were supposed to have been buried with the dead, so that they could hammer on the gates of Purgatory, till the heavenly janitor appeared. Another point to be remembered, and one which we have so often emphasized, is that stone continued to be used after the advent of bronze. Sir William Wilde stated in the middle of the nineteenth century that stone hammers and anvils were used by Irish smiths and tinkers until about that time. Again, Sir John Evans, in *Ancient Stone Implements*, published in 1872, says that up till that time flints were sold in country shops for use with steel to make fire. Leaving the larger imple-ments, we can turn to the lance, javelin, and arrow-heads, and the many things which were made out of the flakes. Long flakes up to 8 and 9 inches were pos-sible, and these were used for lance-heads; shorter ones for javelins and arrows; thicker and rougher flakes for scrapers. Having obtained the flakes, the maker then proceeded to trim these into the desired shape, by what the archaeologists call secondary flaking. In some of the Danish specimens the flaking is rippled along the edge of the implement in a most delightful way. Opinions are divided as to how this secondary flaking was done. However, it is all done by some form of pressure flaking which we saw was invented in the Upper Palaeolithic. A flint punch, or fabricator, may have been used; or the flake held flat, face uppermost on an anvil stone, may have been trimmed by hammering tiny flakes off the edge with a hammer-stone. The Eskimo place the flake over a slight hollow in a log, and then press an ivory tool which spalls off small flakes. Captain John Smith, writing in 1606 of the Indians of Virginia, said: 'His arrow-

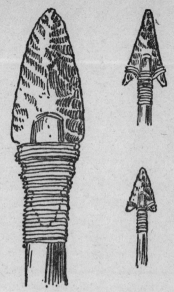

Fig. 6 Flint spear- and arrow-heads

head he maketh quickly with a little bone, which he ever weareth at his bracert (guard on wrist against bow-string), of any splint of stone or glasse in the form of a heart, and these they glew to the end of their arrowes. With the sinewes of deer and the tops of deer's horns boiled to a jelly, they make a glew which will not dissolve in water.' This means a form of mounting as Fig. 6. The arrow-heads must have called for wonderful handling when being made. As with the axes, tradition has gathered round the arrow-heads, which, until quite recent times, were called elf-darts by the country people, who thought that the fairies used them to injure cattle.

Having seen something of the tools which Neolithic man possessed, we can pass on to the work he did with

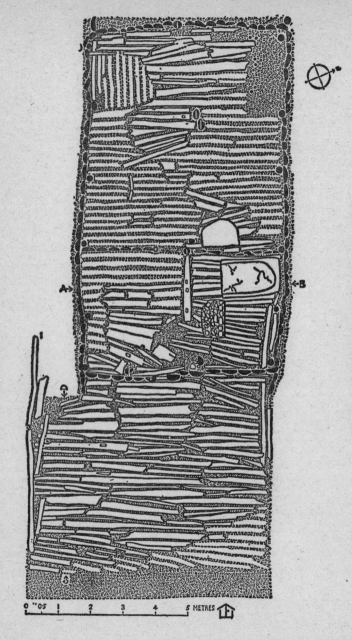

Fig. 7 Plan of a Neolithic house at Aichbuhl

0 "0·5 1 2 3 4 5 METRES

Fig. 8 Aichbuhl Neolithic village

these, and will begin with the houses he built. In Fig. 2 very simple huts are shown which resemble those of the Old Stone Age.

These huts are round and seem to have been used both in England and France during the Neolithic times and also in some of the countries in the Mediterranean. The best British houses of this type were found by accident under the sands at Skara Brae and Rinyo in the Orkney Islands, off the Scottish coast. These islands are quite bare and, as there was no wood to make the houses, they are built of stones. If you go there you can still see the houses, which lead into one another and have stone beds and stone chairs as well as stone fireplaces and stone boxes in which to keep water. Unfortunately very few houses have been found in England. Beneath the earth only one or two holes which once held posts still remain. But at Halden in Devon and also in the Cambridgeshire Fenland enough of these post holes have been found to show that some of the Neolithic houses were square or rectangular. We illustrate a good example of this kind of house from Aichbuhl in Germany, where one or two whole villages of this kind of house were discovered. These were preserved in the ground because it had become wet and boggy before the Neolithic men

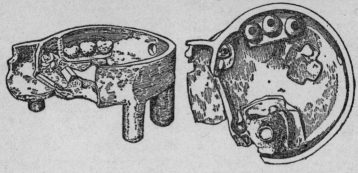

Fig. 9   A Neolithic dolls' house

abandoned it, and so the wood had not all rotted away. In the plan of one of these houses (Fig. 7), you can see that every plank of the floor is still in position. The inside of the house is surrounded by upright wooden planks which were made of logs sawn in half, just like a Canadian log cabin. These are marked on the plan in black. You can see that the house was divided into two rooms, a big one for living in and a small one with a fireplace for cooking. A wall divided these two rooms and if you look carefully you can see the doorway, which has no planks across it. Outside the door of the house is a plank veranda, but there is no outside door visible on the plan. It seems as if there was no way out except by squeezing between the planks. Fig. 8 shows what the excavator thinks a village of these houses must have looked

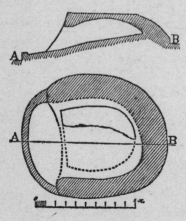

Fig. 10   Plan of a clay oven

like. Some of this
may be guess-work,
but there are ways of
judging a house's
appearance and even
its height from a
complete excavation
of its foundations.

Fig. 11 A clay oven

Another way we can find out about Neolithic houses is from the house models which some of the Neolithic people made for their children. We illustrate a little house on legs also found in Central Europe (Fig. 9). This is a little round house with perhaps a mud wall raised off the ground on wooden piles because it was marshy, like the Swiss Neolithic lake villages, or like the Iron Age dwellings at Glastonbury we will be talking about later. In the house you can see three pits for storing grain and water, and a little man grinding grain in one corner. On the other side of the doorway there is a dome-shaped structure with a flat top like a ladies' hat. This can only be seen in the plan of the house model. We only know what this is because we have dug up the real thing in Neolithic houses in this part of the world. It is a clay oven like that seen in Fig. 11.

Fig. 12 Strike-a-light

We do not know much about the clothes that the men wore who lived in these houses or in those in England.

Flint thumb-scrapers found in the Dartmoor huts suggest skin clothing; though weaving appears to have been started in the Swiss

Fig. 13   A flint sickle

lake dwellings in Neolithic times, it is doubtful if it started here till the Bronze Age. Very few ornaments have been found in long barrows.

Skin clothing does not necessarily mean that Neolithic men only wore the rough pelts of animals. The women of the Old Stone Age could make very good bone needles, and a visit to the Ethnographical Gallery, at the British Museum, will show us what beautiful skin garments the Eskimo can make. Neolithic garments may not have been quite as well made as these. The Picts, who were descendants of the

Fig. 14   Grinding corn

Neolithic men, tattooed themselves, so this method of decoration may have gone back to the New Stone Age.

Fig. 15   Pounding grain

Fig. 12 shows a way that the Neolithic woman made fire; a piece of flint was used, in conjunction with a lump of iron pyrites, as a strike-a-light. Pyrites is found in the lower chalk beds, and may first have been used as a hammer-stone on flint, when the resulting sparks would suggest its use as Fig. 12. The sparks falling on dry moss could be blown into flame. Very beautiful flint knives (Fig. 13), have been found and it is thought that these were used as sickles. The reaper gathered the ears of the corn in one hand, and cut these off as shown. When the corn was cut the threshing was a very simple business, and then came the grinding into flour. Fig. 14 shows a saddle-back quern: the grain was placed on this, in the hollow made by use, and the upper stone pushed to and fro until the corn became flour. Neolithic man would hardly have been able to obtain yeast, and probably his bread was unleavened, or the flour mixed with honey and baked into biscuits. Fig. 15 shows a pot quern, like a modern pestle and mortar, which would have been very useful for pounding things up. These querns were made of gritstone.

We come now to one of the most important discoveries of Neolithic man or woman; he or she found out the way to make pottery. The first pots were made without the use of a potter's wheel, probably in the same way that the Kikuyu of Kenya work today. These people temper their clay by pulling it into small pieces and freeing it from stones; it is then dried in the sun, and afterwards mixed with water until it is plastic. A fine sand is then kneaded into it, in the proportion of about half and half, and the clay finished in long rolls. One or two of these are formed into a collar shape, and with one hand inside this, and the other out, it is gradually modelled into the shape of the top half of the pot, more clay being added in rolls as the work proceeds. The half pot is allowed to dry in the sun for some hours, except the lower edge where the join has to come; this is protected by leaves. This edge has rested on leaves while the top half was being made, so that it could be turned more easily, and this movement must later have suggested the potter's wheel. In the next stage this top half is turned upside down on its already finished mouth, on more leaves, and the modelling proceeds as before, more material being added as required to form the bottom, the shape being given by one hand in, and the other out, until there is only room for one finger, and then the hole is closed, and the pot finished. Again, a few hours are allowed for hardening, then the pots are placed mouth downwards on the ground, and a bonfire of brushwood made all around them; when this has burned out, and the pots are cool, they are ready for use. The only tool used, beside the hand, is a piece of gourd shell.

Fig. 16 Making pottery

Fig. 16 shows how Neolithic

woman went to work, and
Fig. 17 a pottery spoon she
made, which can be seen at
the British Museum.

ABOUT 4¼"

Fig. 17   Pottery spoon

The Kikuyu pottery is made by women, and the
probability is that Neolithic woman did this work, and
looked after the home, while her husband was hunter
and herdsman. She probably did far more than just
cook and mend; we must think of her as an inventor.
With pottery the long train was started which has led
up to the modern saucepan; before then, meat could
only be roasted over a fire, or baked in a cooking-pit,
but with a stout earthen pot that could be placed in
the ashes the Neolithic equivalent of Irish stew was
possible. Water could be heated, and milk and grain
stored.

Perhaps it was the woman who noticed that cattle
ate the seeds of grasses, and experimented by grinding
some between stones; she may have tasted the flour
and found it sweet, and then have brought home more
seeds. A few seeds blew away into the ground newly
turned up at the base of a hut, and the woman watched
these growing and watered and tended them. In this
way it may have occurred to her to make a garden,
and she discovered that cultivation improved the
crop; once this fact was appreciated there were endless
opportunities; the crab apple, wild plum, and other
fruits could be experimented with, and most probably
woman was a gardener before man became a farmer;
of one thing we may be quite sure, Neolithic man did
not rise up one day and plant an acre of ground without endless experiments and questionings going before.

We have seen something of Neolithic houses and the

way Neolithic man lived. He has also left us two types
of monument which are still visible on the surface of
the ground today. These are his cattle camps and his
religious monuments. The cattle camps are the earliest
kind of hill enclosure discovered on the Downs. They
are just a small area of ground on a low flat hilltop
with one, or possibly two, ditches thrown around it.
These ditches provide the earth for a small bank just
inside them which, when it had stakes set along the
top, was sufficient to keep the cattle inside. The ditch
was only a quarry for the earth to form this bank and
when Neolithic man had sufficient earth he did not
bother to dig out the ditch all the way around the hilltop. That is why these camps are called Interrupted
Ditch Camps. Sometimes they are called Causeway
Camps, because there is a causeway between each
section of the ditch that has not been dug out.
Archaeologists think that these camps were used when
the cattle were rounded up in the autumn to be killed
and perhaps salted down. There was little grown in
those days, and there was no way to feed the cattle
through the autumn, so all the bulls except one would
be killed, and perhaps many of the cows too.

We can now pass on to the Neolithic Long Barrow,
or Burial mound, because, apart from its spiritual
significance, which we will discuss later, it has great
interest in its structure. The Long Barrow derives its
name from the fact that it is egg-shaped in plan, and
there are two types; those having chambers inside for
the interment, and others where the bodies were
covered directly by the earth; these latter have a ditch
at the sides leaving a wide path at the original level at
each end. Generally placed east and west, the burial
is usually in the east end, which is higher and broader
than the west. It is a curious fact that the Neolithic

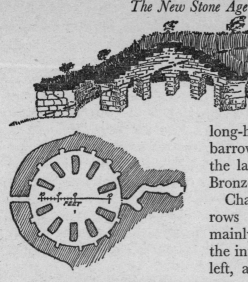

Fig. 18 Earth house, Usinish,
South Uist, Hebrides

long-head built a long barrow, while that of the later round-headed Bronze man was round.

Chambered long barrows are also built mainly of earth, but in the interior a passage is left, and several small rooms or burial chambers are built usually with very large flat blocks of stone. It is the construction of this chamber and corridor, with large stones, which makes it a Megalithic structure, and so links it up with Stonehenge. The building principle is the same, large stones are placed on edge, and the covering formed by others laid flat as lintels. In other structures of this sort, where the span was too great for one stone, courses of masonry were projected from either side as corbels, until the central space was narrow enough to be bridged (*see* Figs. 18 and 19). This is the same method of building as that employed in the Tomb of Agamemnon. Around the outside of the barrow came a dry stone wall with upright sarsen stones at intervals. This dry stone walling was a great accomplishment on the part of the builders, and marked an advance. Long-headed skeletons were sometimes found in these chambers and there is no evidence of cremation. These chambered barrows are planned much on the same lines as the Bronze Age Temples of Malta. Sometimes the bones found in the Long Barrows are disjointed, as if they had been placed there some while after death; and it may well be that only the heroes were thought worthy of such burial. Because the barrows were used for more than one burial, it has been suggested that slaves may have been sacrificed to accompany their tribal chiefs to the spirit world, in the same way that implements and pottery were broken, and animals slaughtered, but it is doubtful if slavery was yet possible. We shall probably be quite safe if we regard these barrows as tribal mausoleums, where the people could assemble and hold services. They are a visible sign to us that Neolithic man believed in a life hereafter, and built them as an emphatic assertion that death is not final. It must have needed some great impulse to bring the tribe together, and make them willing to undertake such a vast work as the construction of a barrow.

This provision of houses for the dead throws an interesting sidelight on the belief of those days; it suggests that in Neolithic times the spirit was tied to the earth for some little while, whereas in the later Bronze Age burials, when the body was burned, it seems as if the spirit was freed at once to go to the spirit-world. The homes for the dead may have been modelled on those of living men; there is a range of

Fig. 19 Picts house, Sutherland (Iron Age)

Fig. 20   Eskimo rock hut

habitations which would appear to have been developments of this idea. Figs. 18 and 19 show what are known as Picts' Houses in Scotland, and this form of stone construction covered with earth is clearly derived from the chambered barrows. Again, the Eskimo houses (Figs. 20, 21) seem to be survivals carried to the north. In Fig. 20 there is a long tunnel entrance leading to the hut, with the beds at A, and the cooking-places at B. The roof of the hut is formed of skins, with a layer of moss between, carried on the poles shown in the sketch. The window is of membrane stretched between whales' jaw bones. The snow house (Fig. 21) is of the same form. There are Picts' houses

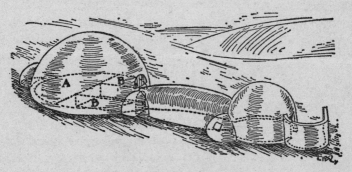

Fig. 21   Eskimo snow house

Fig. 22. Picts' tower (Iron Age)

in Scotland which consist of a paved trench lined with masonry, and covered with stone slabs which terminate in a round chamber.

Fig. 22 shows a Picts' Tower, Doon, or Broch, of a type found in Sutherland, Caithness, Orkneys, Shetlands, and the Hebrides. The little door shown is only 3 feet 8 inches high, by 3 feet broad, and leads through the wall, which is 10 feet 6 inches thick, with a guard cell off the passage 4 feet high and 9 feet long, with a doorway 2 feet square. There is a circular court inside, open to the sky, and in the wall of this, opposite the entrance, another door leads to a passage winding up in the thickness of the wall to upper galleries, all of which are very low, and lighted by windows into the inner court. It is very difficult to date such buildings, but these Picts' towers are Megalithic in character, and built of dry stone;

Fig. 23 A cromlech or dolmen

in design they are first cousins to the Nuraghi of Sardinia, which are fortified dwellings. The Picts are supposed to have descended from the Neolithic stock, and, it may well be, built these towers, perhaps as late as Roman times, in this distant part of the country. Though the earliest Megalithic monuments are built in the Neolithic Period in Britain, this method of building was still in use in the Bronze Age.

Fig. 24   A standing stone

Fig. 23 shows a Cromlech or Dolmen; this was part of the chamber of a barrow, from which the encircling earth has been removed, and ploughed away. Its construction is as described on p. 43.

Fig. 24 shows a Monolith or Standing Stone, called Maen Hir in Wales, where there are many of them. Probably they mark graves of important persons but they sometimes represent the sole relic of a Stone Circle or of an Alignment. The latter is a double parallel row of standing stones, a feature sometimes (as on Dartmoor) extending for more than a mile. It is usually found in connection with the circle or the round barrow and points to religious ceremonial. The

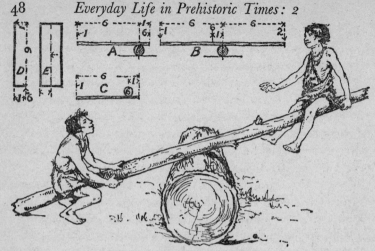

Fig. 25 The laws of leverage

arrangement of one horizontal stone lying across two
uprights, as at Stonehenge, is called a Trilithon.

Megalithic means building with giant stones, and
it is well to realize how large some of these were. Mr.
Peet, in *Rough Stone Monuments*, writes of a block
weighing nearly 40 tons, which must have been
brought 18 miles, at La Perotte, Charente, France.

It may be as well before we pass on to Stonehenge,
the greatest of our Megalithic monuments, to get some
idea of how the builders went to work. It is probable
that the only mechanical aid they had was the lever.
Boys and girls, who learn mechanics, will not need to
be reminded of what the lever means, so they must
excuse this digression for some others who may not
know.

Fig. 25 shows a see-saw, and the principles of
leverage may have been discovered by Neolithic, or
perhaps Palaeolithic, boys and girls amusing themselves in this way. A see-saw is like a pair of scales; it

does not make any difference if you sit on the beam, or are suspended below it. If the two boys sit at an equal distance from the centre, and are of the same weight, they will balance one another, but if one is heavier, he will have to come nearer the centre if equilibrium is to be maintained. So much is this the case, that if he is very much heavier, say 6 stone, to his small brother, 1 stone, then the heavy boy need only be 1 foot from the centre, to balance the light boy at 6 feet (Fig. 25(A)). Imagine the beam at A as a lever; 1 cwt. applied in a downward direction at one end, 6 feet away from the centre, will exert an upward pressure of 6 cwt. at the other end, 1 foot away from the centre.

If the boys sit both on one side, as at B, they will be balanced by a 2-stone boy 6 feet away on the other side. It we take the left-hand side of B, and find that 6 stone at 1 foot = 1 stone at 6 feet, and apply it as at C, and imagine the 6 stone at 1 foot as a log or stone which has to be lifted, then 1-stone lift 6 feet away will do it. We can apply our lever in a different way as at D. The beam is bent at right angles; one arm is 6 feet long, and the short one 1 foot. A 1-stone push at the top of the 6 feet long arm will produce a 6-stone pull up at the end of the horizontal arm, 1 foot long. This brings us to the erection of church steeples, chimney shafts, and towers. Take E, 6 units high, by 2 broad in its base, as a tower which has to resist the pressure of wind by its weight. Wind pressures are known, and their force on the whole area is applied to a lever arm of half the height of the tower as at E. To oppose this there is weight, acting through its centre of gravity, on a lever arm of half the width of the base. If the wind pressure is greater than the weight, over goes the tower. We do not say that primitive man looked at problems in this way, but we do,

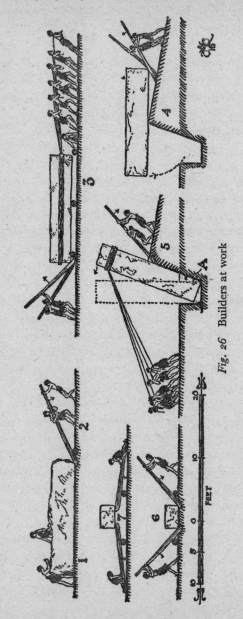

Fig. 26 Builders at work

because of the mechanical laws these early builders discovered.

Bearing these laws in mind, we can pass on to a consideration of how the builders went to work. Nature provided a local sandstone, but the inner circle was constructed of strange stones. The nearest place from which these could have been obtained is the west of Pembrokeshire, and it may be that the stones were already a sacred circle before being moved. Fig. 26(1), shows the masons dressing the stone into shape in its original position to save weight in transport. It is thought that the masons used fire first to heat the stone, and then water to make fragments split off, but it would be a dangerous method, and they may have used wooden wedges instead. We have seen a good mason in Inverness-shire working on a large granite boulder on the hillside where it was dropped out of the bottom of a glacier ages ago. The mason wanted to make a 6-inch landing, and he obtained this by drilling a series of holes, into which he inserted wedges, and so split the landing out of the heart of the boulder. The early men perhaps used the same methods, but of this we cannot be sure; we do know that he had flint and stone tools, because these have been found when excavating to raise the fallen stones at Stonehenge. The flint axes were roughly sharpened, and held in the hand, and appear to have been used to clean the surface of the stone, after it had been bruised by larger stone boulders, or mauls, which smashed off the bumps.

Fig. 26(2) shows men lifting one end of the block to place rollers under it; 3 shows the rollers in position, and men pulling rough hide ropes, with others behind assisting with levers. At 4 we arrive at the building

Fig. 27 Stonehenge

place, where a hole was dug, having one sloping side,
and the upright stone being set in the hole. It was
fixed by ramming small stones into the triangular
space at A 5, but it seems obvious that a sloping
embankment as at 4 must have been built up before
the stone could be tipped into the hole. Without the
embankment it would be nearly impossible to raise the
stone, and a very dangerous job. With the embankment, even if the stone slipped forward a little in the
tipping over, it could easily be levered back into the
hole, and then when resting against the embankment
as at 5, pulling and levering would have raised it;
meanwhile earth shovelled down into the triangular
space at A would have fixed the stone in the desired
position. As to the top lintel stones, these may have
been placed in position by making a bigger embankment, or by levers as 6 and 7. The stone raised once
could be blocked up, and the operation repeated. The
stone shown in Fig. 26 is about the size of one of the
uprights in the outer circle of Stonehenge. First there
is an outer circular ditch and bank, about 300 feet in
diameter. There is an opening on the north-east in the
circle, where it is joined by an avenue. Within this
comes the actual temple. First there is the outer circle,

which originally consisted of 30 stones, standing about
14 feet high by 7 feet wide by 3½ feet thick. Around on
top of these stones comes the circle of crowning lintels,
mortised or hollowed out on their undersides on to
tenons or stubs worked on the tops of the vertical
stones underneath. Fig. 27 gives some idea of what this
outer circle must have looked like when complete.
Within this circle is another, of smaller stones, and
then came five magnificent trilithons arranged in
horseshoe form on plan. Each trilithon consisted of
two upright stones and one lintel, and starting from
the north-east, or entrance side, the height of the
trilithons is increased. Inside the trilithons is another
horseshoe of smaller monoliths, around the flat Altar
stone.

Just inside the entrance from the avenue is a large
flat stone, which has the sombre name of the Slaughter
Stone, and a little way down the avenue another upright one called the Hele Stone.

It may well be that Stonehenge was a temple of the
Sun, from which the priests or medicine men could
take their observation. We accept the longest and
shortest days as a matter of course, if we give the
matter any thought at all, but not so the Neolithic
man. It must have been a mystery to him, that the sun
should appear in a shallow arc across the horizon in
the winter, but climbs into the sky in summer time. It
annoys us on dull days to know that the sun shines
behind the clouds and we cannot see it, and Stonehenge may have been a magic observatory, where the
priests could determine the position of the sunrise
when it could not be seen. The priests may have
settled the seasons; have said now is the time to plant;
now we will sacrifice to the Sun-god that he may make

our crops grow. Again, we accept the miracle of
growth and increase as a commonplace, but the
Neolithic man, who, in one of his rough hand-made
pots, had safeguarded his hardly won seed, did not
commit it to mother earth without some offering, or
propitiation, or sacrifice. The sacrifice was not
necessarily just so much sheer cruelty as an offering to
the gods of some person who was loved, or a pot or
implement which was valuable, so that the person or
family making the sacrifice might be blessed. The
individual did not count for very much in those early
days; the tribe came first, and if one must die to save
the others it had to be. In some such way the sacrifice
became a part of the ritual of early religions. We know
how in Genesis xxii. 2 God said to Abraham, 'Take
now thy son, thine only son Isaac, whom thou lovest,
and get thee into the land of Moriah; and offer him
there for a burnt-offering'.

In the twenty-first book of the *Iliad*, Achilles, after
he has killed the son of Priam, throws him into the
river, and speaking over him 'exalting winged words',
says, 'Nor shall the river avail you anything, fair-
flowing with its silver eddies, though long time have
you made him sacrifice of many bulls, and thrown
down single-hooved horses, still living, into its eddies'.

In Mr. and Mrs. Routledge's book on the Kikuyu
of Kenya, there is an account of the people who dig for
sand for use in making pottery. It is interesting, because it gives us an idea of the spiritual outlook of these
people. The natives tunnel into the hillside for sand,
like so many rabbits, and as they do not take any
precautions, the burrow sooner or later falls in, and
smothers the excavator. The Kikuyu do not take any
steps to dig the poor fellow out, because this would
offend the Spirit of the Sand Pit, but sacrifice a goat

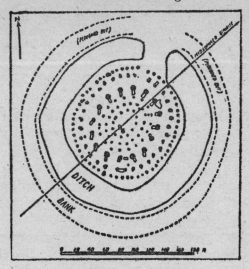

Fig. 28   Plan of 'Woodhenge', Salisbury Plain

instead to propitiate the spirit, then start another burrow which, in its turn, necessitates another goat being sacrificed. This, we think, would have been the case with the Neolithic men: they would worship the Sun, Moon, and Stars, the Rivers and Waters, the Mountains and Valleys, and a great Mother God over all. If by any chance the spirits were offended; if certain things were done which were taboo, or forbidden, sacrifice had to be made.

Stonehenge does not appear to have had any connection with Druidism, which followed many centuries after. The Druids worshipped the Moon and Stars, and Stonehenge was a Sun Temple, built by an agricultural people, to whom the Sun was all-important.

So far as Prehistoric man is concerned, his religion
must have been a very real one to him, or he would not
have taken so much trouble with the Megalithic
monuments we have been describing. These are very
widespread, and can be traced along the shores of the
Mediterranean, through France, to this country; we
have seen how the Picts' towers resemble the Nuraghi
of Sardinia (p. 47), and the chambered barrows the
Stone Age temples of Malta.

The truth is, of course, that the Megalithic monument form was merely a method of building, and
through a great many of the different Megaliths belong
to the New Stone Age, others like Stonehenge belong
to the Early Bronze Age or, like the Picts' towers, may
have been used as a defence against the Romans.

Another type of monument which belongs partly to
the New Stone Age and partly to the Early Bronze Age
is Woodhenge (Fig. 28). This is in the parish of
Durrington, two miles from Stonehenge, and it is the
site of a group of wooden circles. There are socketed
holes of no less than six concentric oval rings of timber
posts, now marked by short concrete pillars. They are
surrounded by a broad, shallow ditch and a flattened
bank beyond. The smaller circle at Arminghall, by
Norwich, also discovered by Wing-Commander Insull,
V.C., has a single horseshoe, once filled by posts
twenty or thirty feet high. They both date from the
time of the Beaker people.

The plan shows the post-holes (black dots) of the
six circles formed by wooden posts at Woodhenge. The
'tabs' attached to the larger dots indicate sloping
ramps (Fig. 26(A)), cut to facilitate the raising of the
posts. The G.P.O. cut similar ramps when raising a
telephone pole. In the centre of the shrine is a grave
in which was found a crouched skeleton facing to-

wards the east with a stone axe-hammer and a beaker (thus establishing a Bronze Age date). Among the finds were two axes made of chalk. These belong to the mystery of the ceremonial. They would have been too soft to use and must have been buried at the outset of the work or the frost would have crumbled them.

This art of building was in its way as wonderful as the La Madeleine paintings, and we must try and imagine the builders. There is a danger in archaeology of thinking more of the things than of the people who made them; we talk of flint implements, as if the New Stone Age could be collected in a bushel basket and shown in the glass cases of a museum, and especially is this the case in the prehistoric period before there was any written history. The interest of things is that they were made by people, and when the things are temples and tombs they become extraordinarily indicative of the spirit of man; of that essence, or aura, which gives him and his work individuality, and has made possible the great works of architecture, painting, poetry, and sculpture, and which makes it possible for a man to lay down his life for an idea. Any great movement which appeals to the minds of men has always been compounded of the spirit.

THE BRONZE AGE

THE MEN of the Upper Palaeolithic found a new material in bone and ivory, and the effect of this was to open up a whole range of new activities. They could make harpoons with barbs in bone, which were not possible with intractable flint. Fishermen should place in their calendar of benefactors the Palaeolithic worker in bone who invented the barb.

Even more so the introduction of metal wrought an enormous difference in the lives of men. The edge of the celt might dull with use, but then it could be hammered up again; it did not fly into fragments, and it could be hammered cold, which is an important detail to remember. Trees could be cut down; houses were built more quickly than was possible before, and in a hundred different ways man was given new confidence in his powers and so was able to make progress.

The discovery of metal was as important in its own way as the introduction of steam, or the discovery of electricity.

We must not think of a Bronze Age which started full blown at a particular date, or of a people who threw away their flint implements one day, to arm themselves with metal on the next. It was a very slow and gradual change-over. It is probable that the first flat celts were brought here by traders from the Continent, and many years may have elapsed before they were followed by the round-headed men we now associate with the Bronze Age, and centuries before the first of the Celtic-speaking peoples who reached this country (*see* p. 26).

The art of Bronze working came from the Near East, by way of Italy and Gaul, and was widely spread, except in Africa, which never had a Bronze Age. We have seen, on p. 26, that the Bronze Age men were more powerful physically than the Mediterranean race. Probably they were not all armed with bronze, but in any case in the end they conquered the Neolithic people. It was not a conquest of extermination, because we find in the round barrows, which are typical of the Bronze Age, round-headed men side by side with long-headed Mediterranean men.

A parallel can be found in Greece, where the Achaeans of the Heroic Age dispossessed the Minoans of Mediterranean stock.

As the art of metal working is the great central fact which has given the name of the Bronze Age to this period, it may be as well to start with a description of the methods followed by prehistoric man in his craft; in doing so we must try and place ourselves in his position, and imagine that we have never seen metal before. Bronze, we know, is an alloy of copper and tin, and we shall find that copper, like gold, is sometimes found almost pure, and is capable of being hammered up cold, without any preliminary smelting to reduce the ores. Iron ore is found in the form of red earth, or stone, and is not so obviously metallic, and would more easily have escaped attention than copper. The North American Indians hammered up pure copper, and made knives in this way before the coming of the European invaders. So the age of bronze may have been preceded by one of copper. Even when smelting and casting bronze had been discovered, it was found that it could be forged cold, and that when it was heated, it tended to become brittle and fly to pieces when being hammered. It is hardened by hammering, and softened by heating and quenching, whereas iron hardens by heating and quenching. Bronze was an ideal metal for prehistoric man, because dulled edges could be hammered up again anywhere without very much trouble. It can be made extremely hard.

We can now pass to smelting. Pottery had given man the idea of taking a plastic material and shaping it; he may have used clay to line a cooking-pit, and found that baking hardened it. In the same way the accidental introduction of copper ore into a cooking-pit, or a charcoal fire exposed to the wind, would have melted the ore, and this would have been found as metal when the ashes were raked aside. The metal may have cast itself into a shape which suggested a tool or weapon, and it would have prompted the ingenious man to experiment. In some such way it must have come about. The first moulds were simple flat open moulds, into which the molten metal could be poured, then progression was made to hollow casting with clay cores which could afterwards be scraped out. Stone, bronze, and probably fine sand were used, and actual moulds can be seen at the British Museum.

We get an inkling of how the Bronze Age men went to work from the *Iliad*, xviii. Hephaistos, the famed artificer, who 'wrought much cunning work of bronze, brooches and spiral arm-bands, and cups and necklaces', when he starts work on the wonderful shield for Achilles – 'went unto his bellows and turned them upon the fire and bade them work. And the bellows, twenty in all, blew on the crucibles, sending deft blasts on every side. . . . And he threw bronze that weareth not into the fire, and tin and precious gold and silver.'

This would have been an apparatus very similar to that used for iron at the Glastonbury lake village (Fig. 60). Copper melts at 1083° centigrade, and tin at only 232°, so that the Bronze Age founder melted the copper first, then threw charcoal on to the melted mass to retain the heat, and added the tin. The ideal aimed at seems to have been 10 per cent tin to 90 per cent copper, but endless experiments went to the discovery that this made a good bronze. Prehistoric man did not know anything about analytical metallurgy. Surface copper ores sometimes contain tin-oxide, and the intelligent man would soon have been moved to find out why an axe made from this ore was tougher than one of pure copper.

Fig. 29 Development of Bronze axe

We can now discuss the actual implements made, and Fig. 29 shows the development of the Bronze Axe. No. 1 is called the Flat Celt, and is obviously fashioned on the lines of the stone axe which preceded it, and was hafted in the same way as Fig. 30. The makers soon discovered that by hammering the edge it became thinner, keener, and wider so the upper part of the later celts is narrower.

Fig. 30   Hafting of palstave and
socketed axe

No. 2 (Fig. 29) shows the Flanged Axe, formed by hammering over the sides. This was hafted as Fig. 30(1). A stick with a stout branch was selected, and this being cut off, was forked to fit over the top of the axe, and bound to it by raw hide. The disadvantage was that the thin axe split the wood head. A stop ridge was then developed between the flanges, and this finally developed into Fig. 29(3), which is known as a palstave, from an Icelandic word for a narrow spud. This stop ridge took the force of the blow, and prevented the head from splitting (Fig. 30(1)). In this type, the web between the flanges, above the stop ridge, was thinner than the axe part under, and this feature is more pronounced in Fig. 29(4), where the flanges are hammered over into the form of what is known as the Winged Axe. No. 5 (Fig. 29) shows the wings lapping, and in 6 they have disappeared, and we arrive at the final Socketed Axe, which was hafted as Fig. 30(2). There were endless intermediates, and the axe is well worth studying, because it is the ancestor of the tool which is still in use today.

The Bronze Spear is a weapon with an interesting history. It started life as Fig. 31(1), and in this form was used either as a knife or a dagger. It was cast solid, and provided with a tang which was fitted into the end of the wooden shaft, and this latter was prevented from splitting by a plain bronze collar, through which a rivet passed and secured the end of the tang. In Fig. 31(2) the collar has become socket-shaped, and though not cast with the spear-head, is attached to it by two rivets, and the tang still remains. In Fig. 31(3)

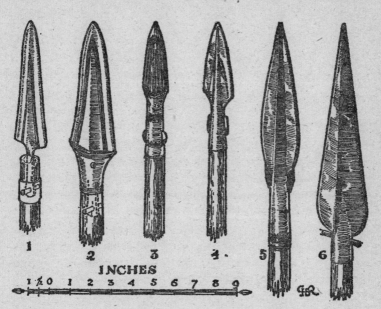

Fig. 31 Development of Bronze spear

the tang has gone, and the socket is part and parcel of the spear-head. But an amusing fact should be noticed: that the rivets which once fastened it to the head remain as ornamental bumps; Fig. 31(3) has loops for thong attachment to the shaft, or for tying on feathers or streamers. In Fig. 31(4 and 5) the socket has further developed, and the spear-head is formed of fins cast on to the sides of the socket. In Fig. 31(5) these are leaf-shaped, and the loops are decorative. In Fig. 31(6) the whole spear-head is a triumph of hollow casting.

The sword developed out of the knife by way of the dagger or rapier. It is easy to see that spear-head No. 1 (Fig. 31), if it had a short handle fitted on to the tang instead of the shaft, would make a useful knife. A rapier was an elongated dagger, and the sword a later invention. Fig. 32 shows a beautiful leaf-shaped

Fig. 32 A leaf-shaped sword

sword. The tang for the handle was cast on the blade, with the edges slightly flanged up, and then in between these edges grips of horn or wood were riveted on each side through the tang, and a round pommel clipped on to the end. Leather scabbards were used with bronze tips called chapes. Bronze was not used for arrowheads, but flint, as in Neolithic times. The two drawings, Fig. 29 of the axes, and Fig. 31 of the spears, show the development over the whole of the Bronze Age, and this lasted not less than 1300 years. To realize how long a time this is, we must remember that 1300 years ago in this country would take us back nearly to the time of the

Fig. 33 A Bronze Age smith

death of Ethelbert, king of the Kentish men, and the first English king who received baptism.

These swords and spears are the beginning of the history of Arms and Armour. In the Stone Age men were probably, like the Eskimo, so engaged in finding enough to eat that little time was left for quarrelling about their scanty possessions. With the introduction of metals they could make more things, and life became easier and they had more time for fighting. These Bronze Age arms must have been used in the way described in the *Iliad*.

A flanged axe with slight stop ridge, a type midway between 2 and 3, Fig. 29, was found with a spear-head slightly earlier in form than Fig. 31(3). The archaeologist in this way, by associated finds, builds up a theory of the dates and developments of civilizations. Fig. 33, drawn from the actual tools at the British Museum, shows the equipment of a Bronze Age metalworker. At 1 are his hammers, hafted like socketed axes; 2 shows a tanged chisel, and 3 a socketed gouge; 4 is a sandstone rubber, and 5 an anvil.

One of the most interesting discoveries ever made in England was what appears to be the complete furnishing of a family at the end of the Bronze Age. This was found in Heathery Burn Cave, County Durham, which may have been used as a house, or as a place of refuge. From remains of skulls which were discovered, the inhabitants appear to have been long-headed men of Mediterranean or Neolithic stock, and it is possible that they removed to the cave in face of the danger of invasion. We shall see later how, at Glastonbury, a people of similar extraction were put to the sword by invaders.

The Heathery Burn discovery included a sword

much the same as Fig. 32, but with slight shoulders on the cutting edge of the blade near the handle; a leaf-shaped spear-head, as Fig. 31(5), but without the loops; bronze discs 5 inches diameter, which may have been used as dress ornaments or horse trappings; bronze collars which fitted on to the nave or hub of chariot wheels, and which, in conjunction with the bridle bit, show that the horse was used. A bucket was found, and tanged and socketed knives; a razor, a gouge, and a socketed axe as Fig. 29(6), chisels, awls, pins, rings, tongs, and gold armlets. There were bone prickers, spindle whorls, skewers, knives, the cheek-bars of bridle-bits, and jet armlets; and all these things can be seen at the British Museum. This splendid find includes nearly all the known types of Bronze Age implements, and we have founded our illustrations on these Heathery Burn discoveries.

Fig. 34 Bronze brooch and pin

The spindle whorl shows that spinning was practised in the Bronze Age in this country; both spinning and weaving are supposed to have started in the Swiss lake dwellings as early as the Neolithic times. Various types of dress fastenings began to come into use which were suitable for light woven fabrics. Fig. 34 shows a bronze brooch from Ireland, shaped rather like a large hollow curtain-ring, and so arranged that a bronze pin could be passed through it, and in this way fasten a cloak drawn through the ring. This type may have suggested the penannular brooch (Fig. 63).

In a barrow of this period in the

East Riding of Yorkshire, the remains of a linen winding-sheet were found under a skeleton, and woollen fabrics have been found in others; these could only have been woven on a loom. We will consider, then, the steps which a Bronze Age weaver had to take if she wished to convert a fleece into a piece of stuff for making clothes. It would need washing and cleansing first, and then came dyeing. Crotal, a lichen growing on trees, may have been used. If this is put in a pot with the fleece and water, and boiled for one or two hours, it produces a rich red-brown colour.

Fig. 35 Spinning

Teasing consists of pulling the fleece into fluff, and oiling explains itself. Carding is an operation which consists of putting the wool on an implement rather like a large butter-pat with teeth, called the card, and then pulling the other card across it, so as to arrange the wool for spinning. This latter was the occupation of girls for so many centuries, that we still talk of an unmarried woman as a spinster.

The spindle which was used in the Bronze Age consisted of a piece of wood, perhaps about 1 foot long and $\frac{1}{2}$ inch diameter, and a few inches from one end came the whorl, which acted as a miniature fly-wheel and helped to twist the spindle. At the other end was a little nick in which the yarn was fastened. In spinning, a roll of carded wool was held in the left hand, or bound on to a distaff; from this roll a little wool was

T–C

pulled out and twisted by the fingers until a piece of
yarn was made about 18 inches long, and this was
tied to the spindle. The wool was then paid out with
the left hand, and the spindle twisted with the right.
When the spindle stopped revolving it was held, when
the twist ran up the length of wool which had been
paid out and made this into yarn, which could then
be wound on to the spindle and the spinning resumed
(Fig. 35).

Weaving is, and has been since the Bronze Age, one
of the crafts which has had the greatest influence on
the progress of man. It is beautiful work, done where-
ever man wants clothes, and carried out in many
different ways; but the main principle of weaving is
always the same. The long threads running through
the length of a piece of cloth are called the warp; the
ones which cross these by
going under and over the
warp are called the weft.
From the discovery of loom
weights, as shown at the
bottom of the warp-threads
in Fig. 36, in the Swiss lake
villages and in England,
it is thought that the earliest looms were of this pattern, which is called the
Warp-weighted Loom – the
weights keeping the warp
properly stretched. The
warp-threads were kept in
place by yarn threaded
through them at the bot-
tom. It is probable that at

Fig. 36 Warp-weighted loom of
simplest type

first the weaver took the skein of yarn in her right hand, and picking up the warp-threads one or two at a time with the left hand, passed the weft-threads through from side to side, over and under the warp. She may have used a wooden lath to beat the weft-threads up, and so make the cloth compact.

Fig. 37 shows the next development, and our drawing is based on the Scandinavian loom in the Copenhagen Museum. The diagrams at the side, A and B, illustrate the method of weaving, and we shall find as we go along that, though the details are elaborated, this principle remains. A piece of fabric has been woven from the top downwards, and below this the warp-strings hang down with their weights on the ends. They are divided at 1 by a shed-stick: the

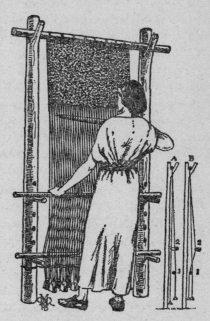

Fig. 37   Warp-weighted loom of more developed type

shed is the space through which the weft is passed. At 2 is the heddle-rod, which is attached to alternate warp-strings by loops. The weaver then passes his shuttle through the space between the warp-strings, above the heddle-rod in A position, which is called the counter shed. The heddle-rod is then pulled out to B position, which brings the warp-threads which were at the back to the front, and the weft is again passed through the space now called the shed.

In this way the weaving proceeds, like darning, first under and over the warp-strings, then over and under. This would make a plain cloth; in patterned work different coloured yarns can be used, and instead of just over and under the warp, you can go over and under and then skip two or three, and so produce a pattern. On Greek vases Penelope is shown working at an upright warp-weighted loom like Fig. 37, but it has been developed by making the top cloth beam to revolve, so that the cloth could be wound up as it is woven.

Fig. 38
A comb

Fig. 38 shows what is called now a weaver's comb, found at Glastonbury lake village, but we doubt if this was used, as suggested, to comb or pack the weft-threads tightly together; it would have been an inconvenient way of doing it; so here is a problem for our readers to determine the use of the comb.

Fig. 39 is taken from a Bronze Age drawing on the side of a bronze vessel. This is very hard to understand since it is drawn in straight lines, but if you look very carefully you will see three triangular women engaged in spinning and in weaving with just the same sort of loom as we have drawn for you. The remains of dresses of this period have been found in Jutland, which suggest that the piece of stuff woven on the looms was wrapped around the body without any shaping. This is the case with the tunic of the man and the skirt of the girl. In the case of the man this was the beginning of the kilt. The girl's bodice would have

Fig. 39   A Bronze Age drawing of women weaving

been roughly cut in kimono shape, and the side seams sewn under the arms. She might wear a bronze disc fastened on to a woven tas-selled belt, with her hair gathered into a thread net, and fastened by long bronze pins. The shoes of both man and woman were of skin, and the man had a circular cloak and cap of thick rough knotted wool.

Fig. 40 shows a man shaving with a razor of a very usual pattern in England during the Bronze Age; he probably used oil instead of soap.

We have seen on p. 65 that one of the finds at the Heathery Burn Cave was a point of deer antler, about

Fig. 40   Shaving with Bronze razor

five inches long and curved in shape; it is pierced twice on the radial lines of the curve, and once at right angles. Similar pieces have been found in the Swiss lake dwellings, and it is suggested that these were the cheek-bars of bridle-bits. Probably the first bit was a twisted leather thong, knotted at the width of the mouth, and then the ends passed through the cheek-pieces as reins. If the transverse hole of one of these horn bars is examined, it will be found to be worn smooth as by a leather rein. Similar cheek-pieces are described in the *Iliad*.

The Heathery Burn discovery includes bronze nave collars for chariot wheels. The nave of a wheel is its hub, and this suggests spokes. The first wheels were probably solid on their axle, rather like a cotton reel. Fig. 41(A) shows another type made up of three boards secured by dovetailed clamps. Fig. 41(B) shows the start of the spoke, not as we know it today, but arranged more as a brace. The upright part includes nave, two spokes, and parts of the felly or rim, all in one piece of wood. The four other spokes are braced between this and the remaining parts of the felly. These came from the Swiss lake dwellings, and must be early types, because a later wheel has been found there which, though in bronze, must have been founded on a wooden construction. It is $19\frac{3}{4}$ inches in diameter, and has four spokes radiating between nave and fellies, just like the wheel of today. We know too that beautifully turned wooden wheel naves have been found at Glastonbury lake village, dating from the Early Iron Age, and in what are called the chariot burials of Yorkshire, of the same period, the iron tyres of chariot wheels have been discovered.

The original Aryan-speaking peoples, the fore-runners of the Celts, are supposed to have possessed ox-

wagons, and it may well be that
chariots were introduced into England during the Late Bronze Age
between 700 and 500 B.C.

It is interesting to see the drawings
Bronze Age men did of these chariots. We illustrate two of these
drawings (Figs. 42, 43). The first,
scratched on a broken piece of pottery, shows a chariot used in a funeral. The dead man has been burnt
and put in a large container on the
chariot. The chariot is drawn by
two horses and the dead man's
charger is being led in front of the
chariot, just like the Duke of Well-
ington's charger that carried him at
Waterloo was led at his funeral a

2' 0" diam.

2' 10" diam.

Fig. 41 Wooden
wheels

hundred years ago. The second drawing is a rock
carving showing two-wheel war chariots, and a four-
wheel cart drawn from above. The artist did not know
how to draw the wheels properly in this position, so
they are placed sideways so that you can recognize
them.

The chariot does not give very much opportunity
to the maker to vary its shape. There must be a floor
framed up on the axle, around which would come the
body, perhaps of wickerwork covered with hides.
There would have been a centre pole, with yoke
attachment to the horses. The chariot of classical
times must have been founded on some such simple
basis. Again we cannot do better than turn to the
Iliad for an idea of how chariots were used.

This question of wheel naves, the discovery of jet
armlets at Heathery Burn Cave, and shale cups in

Fig. 42   A funeral procession engraved on a piece of broken pottery

round barrows, all of which must have been turned,
brings up the question of lathes. It is difficult to see
how a simpler turning contrivance than the pole
lathe (Fig. 65) could be made, and this may date from
the Bronze Age.

We know little of the tracks these chariots must have
used, though Bronze Age Corduroy-roads of planks
have been found preserved in the marsh peats of East
Anglia, and fords may have been replaced by bridges;
there are two on Dartmoor which are still called
Celtic. Fig. 44 shows one of these at Postbridge, and
its construction is just what we should expect from a
people who had inherited the building tradition of
Stonehenge. We should like to draw attention to the

Fig. 43   A rock engraving of two chariots and a four-wheel cart

Fig. 44 A clapper bridge

trumpet shown in the hands of one of the figures.
These instruments derive their shape from the horns
of animals, which had been used for the same purpose
before. They were made at the end of the Bronze Age,
in that metal, and are supposed to have been used by
the Celtic people in warfare; of two types, some have
the mouthpiece at the side.

The possession of the bronze axe, with its better
cutting powers, meant that man could make ever
larger clearings in the forest, grow more corn, and
keep more herds. He was helped again, because with
his bronze sickle the harvesting of his crops was not
such a problem as when that useful implement was of
flint (Fig. 13). There is a beautiful harvest scene in the
eighteenth book of the *Iliad* – 'where hinds were reap-
ing with sharp sickles in their hands. Some armfuls
along the swathe were falling in rows to the earth,
while others the sheaf-binders were binding in twisted
bands of straw. Three sheaf-binders stood over them,
while behind boys gathering corn and bearing it in

Fig. 45   A plough

their arms gave it constantly to the binders; and among them the king in silence was standing at the swathe with his staff, rejoicing in his heart. And henchmen apart beneath an oak were making ready a feast, and preparing a great ox they had sacrificed; while the women were strewing much white barley to be a supper for the hinds.' Game was less eaten now than the domesticated animals; a proof that life was becoming easier, and it was not

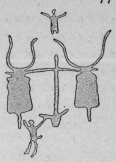

Fig 46 Rock engraving of a man ploughing with oxen, as seen from above

necessary to live by the chase. There are Scandinavian and Ligurian rock carvings of Bronze Age date, which show a primitive plough drawn by oxen. One of these which we have copied for you, shows an aerial view or plan of a man ploughing with two oxen (Fig. 46). You can see the plough in his hand, and another man in front shouting to the oxen to hurry them up. Archaeologists believe that the introduction of the plough is the greatest change that took place in prehistoric times after the discovery of farming. The plough came into Britain in late Bronze Age times just before the introduction of iron. At the same time the first real fields are discovered – the little *Celtic Fields* still seen on the Salisbury Plain – and the population in England increased about ten times in this period. This is because the introduction of the plough made farming more efficient – much more corn could be gathered from the fields, and so more and more people could live in Britain.

Pottery was still hand-made, without a wheel, but ornament was improving, and consisted of straight

Fig. 47 Bronze Age pottery ornament

lines arranged as chevrons, lozenges, herring-bones, with dots and concentric circles (Fig. 47). Fig 48(1) is of a beaker, or drinking-vessel, which was introduced on the East Coast by the Beaker people (*see* p. 26); it is found with unburnt burials; 2 is a food vessel; 3 a cinerary urn, made to hold the ashes of a cremated burial; and 4 an incense cup. This does not mean that the Bronze Age people used incense, and the name has been suggested by the pierced treatment of the little cups; these are found in round barrows, and may have been used to bring the sacred fire which started the funeral pyre. It is thought that these types of pottery, which were doubtless deposited with the dead, for their use in the spirit world, are similar to those they used in their everyday life. Bronze implements were buried for the same reason, but were generally limited to plain axes, knife, daggers, and awls, and this limitation points to some symbolical meaning in those selected.

Burial was either by burying the body (inhumation),

or by burning it (cremation), and it is a little bewilder-
ing to find both methods practised at the same time,
because inhumation is distinctly Neolithic, and cremation a Celtic custom, and yet this latter was practised
before the Celts arrived. This points to a survival of the
long-headed people and their ways, and the introduction of cremation as a fashion by the earlier round-
heads from the Continent. A pit was dug in the ground,
and a stone cist was made of four stones on edge
covered by another, or a hole cut in the chalk, and the
ground heaped over in the form of a round barrow. In
a stone country, the barrow was made of heaped
stones, and became a cairn. Fig. 49(1) is the type
which is called a Bowl Barrow, because it is like an
inverted bowl; (2) a Bell Barrow, because the ditch
and bank made around the outside give it that shape;
and (3) is a Disc Barrow.

A barrow is sometimes called a Tumulus; in Derbyshire, a Low; and in Yorkshire, a Howe.

Silbury Hill, 6 miles west of Marlborough, on the
Bath Road, is in the form of a round barrow, but it is
135 feet high, and covers 6 acres. It is wholly artificial,
and in 1907, at the rates of pay then obtaining, its
cost was estimated at £20,000.

Cup and ring markings are common on the cover
stones of the cists or graves in the barrows, and these
are very similar to the markings found on the *churingas*
of the Australian aborigines.

Small objects called Sun Discs are found in Ireland;
these are made of gold about $2\frac{3}{4}$ inches diameter, and
have the same decorative idea as the cup and ring
markings, made up of concentric circles. All these
things point to Sun-worship being characteristic of the
Bronze Age; another symbol, which is widely distri-
buted, is the swastika, also considered a symbol of the Sun.

It must be borne in mind that prehistoric man was still held in thrall by magic and mystery; that there were many things which were taboo or forbidden; like the Kikuyu his life and death were governed by a complicated ritual. Cremation in all probability was not practised to destroy the body, but to purify it of

Fig. 48   Bronze Age pottery

sins and uncleanness, and render the spirit fit for the life hereafter. In the twenty-third book of the *Iliad* the spirit of the hapless Patroklos appears to Achilles and urges him: 'Thou sleepest and hast forgotten me, Achilles. While I lived never did'st thou forget me, and only now that I am dead. Bury me with all despatch, so that I may pass the gate of Hades. Far do the spirits keep me off, the spirits of men out-worn; they suffer not that I should join their company beyond the River; and vain are my wanderings through the wide-gated house of Hades. Pitifully I beg that thou

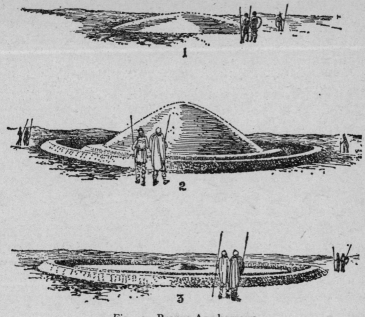

Fig. 49 Bronze Age barrows

should'st give me thy hand; never again shall I come
back from Hades, once you have granted me my due
of fire.' We have seen that the implements which were
buried with Bronze Age man were limited to certain
symbolical types. Again we find that in the actual
cinerary urns were buried, with the human remains,
the bones of wild animals, like the fox, mole, and
mouse; surely these typified something. In the barrow
itself, the bones of the ox, goat, sheep, horse, pig, and
dog have been found with cremated burials; of these
some may be the remains of the funeral feasts, and the
horse and dog may have been slaughtered to accompany their master, and the sacrifice of slaves and captives may have formed part of the ceremony. Bone
pins have been found, charred by fire, as if they had

fastened the body in its shroud before it was burned.

Homer, in the twenty-fourth book of the *Iliad*, gives a wonderful picture of the burial of Hector:

'So nine days they gathered great store of wood. But when the tenth morn rose with light for men, then bare they forth brave Hector, weeping tears, and on a lofty pyre they laid the dead man, and thereon cast fire.

'But when the young dawn shone forth, rosy-fingered Morning, then gathered the people round glorious Hector's pyre. Assembling, they first of all quenched the flames of the pyre with wine, even as far as the might of the flames had reached, and thereupon his brethren and friends gathered his white bones, mourning him with big tears coursing down their cheeks. The bones they took and laid away in a golden urn, wrapping them up in soft purple robes, and quickly set the urn in a hollow grave, and heaped above great stones, closely placed. Then hastily they piled a barrow, while everywhere about watchers were posted, through fear that the well-greaved Achaians might make an onslaught before the time. And, when the barrow was piled, they went back and, assembling, duly feasted and well in the palace of Priam, that king fostered by Zeus. Thus did they hold funeral for Hector, tamer of horses.'

In the twenty-third Book even fuller details are given of the funeral of Patroklos, and the funeral games – of how they went forth 'to hew high-foliaged oaks with the long-edged bronze', and 'splitting them asunder the Achaians bound them behind mules', and so brought the wood to the appointed place, and made a great pile. 'And they heaped all the corpse with their hair that they cut off and threw thereon.' The pyre was 'a hundred feet this way and that, and on the pyre's top set the corpse'. 'And many lusty sheep and shambling crook-horned oxen they flayed and made ready before the pyre; and taking from all of them the fat, great-hearted Achilles wrapped the corpse therein from head to foot, and heaped the flayed bodies round. And he set therein two-handled jars of honey and oil, leaning them against the bier; and four strong-necked horses he threw swiftly on the pyre, and groaned aloud. Nine house-dogs had the dead chief: of them did Achilles slay twain and threw them on the pyre. And twelve valiant sons of great-hearted Trojans he slew with the sword' to be consumed by the fire. The North Wind and the loud West 'all night drave they the flame of the pyre together, blowing shrill', and after a barrow was made as already described for the burial of Hector. Then followed the funeral games, of which all can read in the twenty-third book of the *Iliad*. The next time we see a round barrow, we must think of it, not as only so much heaped earth, but rather as a visible sign of our own Heroic Age. We must try and conjure up a picture of the flaming pyre, and looking across the smoking eddies of time, see the crowd of Bronze Age warriors burying their chief.

Figs. 50, 51, and 52 show the remarkable and extensive early Bronze Age tumulus of Bryn Celli Dhu, another variety of burial monument in use at this time. There was a large outer circle of standing stones (now gone). This was in full view. The three other circles were hidden in the mound covering the burial chamber. The two next circles indicated by heavy black and light broken lines (Fig. 50) consist of upright stones with dry stone walling between them. Actually they are not circles for, when traced out from end to end (including the passage and chamber in the heart of the mound) they are found to form a con-

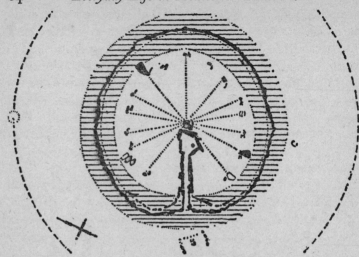

Fig. 50 Plan of the chambered cairn of
Bryn Celli Dhu, Anglesey

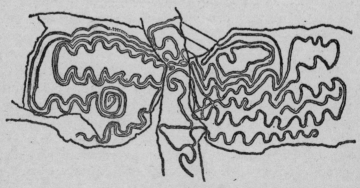

Fig. 51 Diagram of markings on the pattern stone,
Bryn Celli Dhu

tinuous spiral – a magic cypher! The innermost circle
is of single stones. At the foot of some of them the
burned bones of young persons were found. The
dotted lines connecting them show how they are
arranged in opposite pairs in line with the centre of the
whole tomb. To one side of the inner chamber will be
noticed a recess to make room for the black dot. That
dot is a tooled pillar standing five foot six inches above
ground (Fig. 52). The stone
with the design illustrated in
Fig. 51 is shown just beyond
the chamber and by it an-
other at the very centre of
the whole tomb. This covered
a small pit containing two
large lumps of red jasper.
Just outside the entrance to
the passage was the skeleton
of an ox, its head turned towards the portal. The Min-
istry of Works has restored

Fig. 52   Pillar stone in chamber
of Bryn Celli Dhu

the chamber and the covering-mound. The date is
about 1500 B.C., and the monument seems to represent
the amalgamation of many cults of the circle and the
barrow.

We will now try to give our readers some idea of the
migrations and minglings, the traffic and trade routes,
which had developed in the Bronze Age from the
earlier Neolithic beginnings. We must first ask ourselves why it is we find these big movements of men,
because, leaving on one side the adventurous few, the
general run of people do not move until they are
pushed. In the Old Stone Age, man moved because he
was a hunter, and had to follow the chase to live, and

in the same way, even when he had settled down, he could not be sure of a permanent home, unless it was accompanied by a perennial food supply; if this failed, then he had to break fresh ground. If food were one of the reasons for his moving, he naturally went away from the crowded central area, or falling on his neighbours compelled them to do so. Wars have played a terrible part in migrations; we have seen in our time great movements of people, as a result of the 1939–45 struggle. The study of these movements is of great value as bearing on the original homes of men. That is why the archaeologists continually do dig; they are hunting for first causes.

Geography will help us to discover the natural causes of man's movements on certain lines. Loess land is a sandy, chalky loam, deposited at first as dust blown by great blizzards from the glaciers in the Ice Ages. This loess is in a broad zone, which, starting from the Ural Mountains, stretches across South Russia to the Carpathians, and the Danube, then through north-west Austria to south Germany, and the north of France. The fine grain of the loess prevented the spread of forests, and became instead the great grasslands which have played so considerable a part in the development of Europe. Here have been bred great hordes of men, who in times of drought, or when the regions became overpopulated, have descended on the ancient civilization of the East, and caused movements of men. In the same way, the Arabian Desert has been a great reservoir of hardy people, who periodically have made exodus, with terrible happenings to their prosperous neighbours, or have been bribed to keep the peace.

The problem which confronts such a people is similar to that of the hill-tribes of the North-West frontier of India. Here the Mohmands, Afridis, Wazirs, and Mahsuds, perched on the barren hills, can only live by levying tribute on the caravans passing from the fat lands. Here through the great land gate of the Khyber Pass, through all the ages, immigrants have gone into India. The Aryans, and Alexander: all travelled on this line until a new way was forced by sea.

If along a certain line similar kinds of pottery or stone monuments are found, it is fair to assume that these are the work of a particular type of people moving along this line. If in Bronze Age barrows we find gold from Ireland, glass or beads from the Mediterranean, amber from Scandinavia, or in an Early Iron Age cemetery at Aylesford in Kent, a bronze flagon from north Italy, it points to trade and trade routes. We may be sure that salt was traded.

We have already written, on p. 24, of one of the earliest migrations, that of the Mediterranean people; also of the first of the round-heads, and of the arrival of the Beaker people; and, on p. 26, of the movements of the Aryan-speaking peoples. This brings up another factor of great importance in the lives of men, and one which is not concerned so much with their movements, as with the circulation of some great idea that acted as a lever, and caused them to alter their mode of living. The wonderful drawings and paintings of the Aurignac and La Madeleine Periods in the Old Stone Age, and the Megalithic buildings of the New Stone Age, were wrought around some central inspiration; again, in the latter half of the Bronze Age, the prophets were at work, and we find the introduction, by the Aryan-speaking peoples, of cremation and all that it may have implied. The Minoan civilization was centred in the island of Crete, the home of Minos, and then transferred to Mycenae on the mainland of

Greece. The Cretans were of the Mediterranean stock; their power declined about the 1500th century B.C. Their buildings were Megalithic, and they did not cremate their dead. While the Minoan civilization was dying, we hear of the beginnings of the Heroic Period of the Hellenes. Jason, Agamemnon, Hector, and Odysseus are typical of wild men who came from the north, finding their way down from the grasslands, and they were an Aryan-speaking people who cremated their dead. The Achaeans were followed by the Dorians, who destroyed the Mycenaen civilization in Greece, and settling down became the Spartans. There were great movements of the Celts, Gaels, or Gauls, in the Early Iron Age. They were a Nordic people living to the north of the Alps, and called by the Romans for this reason Transalpine. They sacked Rome in 395 B.C., and were typical of the barbarians across the Danube and Rhine who were to become a constant menace to the Empire later on.

If the Mediterranean men found their way through Gaul, a later route seems to have been from Marseilles (Massilia) by the Rhône Valley to Châlons, where it divided into three lines; one to the west down the Loire, the second around the Paris basin, and the third through the Belfort Gap, between the Vosges and Jura Mountains, and down the Rhine. This latter route is an important one, because it mingled people coming up from the Mediterranean with another type coming from the regions to the north of the European and Asiatic Mountains.

Professor Fleure thinks that the Beaker people came from Kiev on the Dnieper, south of the Pinsk Marshes. Their settlements have been found on the tributaries of the March in Moravia; on the Bohemian tributaries of the Elbe by Prague; around the junction of the Saale and Elbe; the mouth of the Oder; on the Zuyder Zee; and again at the junction of the Rhine and Main. In the British Isles pottery beakers of the same type are found on our eastern coasts from Caithness to Kent, and also found on the west coast of Scotland.

The west coast of Denmark, and the south Baltic, supplied amber during the Bronze Age, and the two main trade routes pass through Germany to the Adriatic. One started from Venice, up the valley of the Adige, through the Brenner Pass, down the Inn to Passau on the Danube, and then by way of the Moldau to the Elbe, and so to Denmark. The second route was from Trieste to Laibach and Graz, then to Pressburg on the Danube, from there up the River March, across Moravia and through Silesia, along the Oder, then across Posen to the Vistula, and Danzig. The spiral design of the Bronze Age found in Scotland, Cumberland, Lancashire, Northumberland, south Ireland, and Merionethshire, and which was common in Egyptian and Ægean art, is supposed to have found its way here on the first of these two routes.

We can now pass from land journeys to sea voyages, and we will work back from Caesar's time. It was the Veneti, maritime tribesmen occupying what is now Vannes, Morbihan, in Brittany, who formed a confederation of the tribes in north and north-west Gaul against the Romans. The Veneti seem to have controlled the trade with Britain, and possessed a fleet of large ships with leathern sails, high poops, and towers, but did not use oars, which was the reason they were beaten on a calm day by the Romans.

If we go back again to the time of Pytheas of Marseilles, about 330 B.C., we find that he sailed to Britain, and there was in his time a regular trade between Cornwall and Marseilles, and probably a sea-borne trade between Cornwall and Cadiz (Gades) which was a centre of the tin trade. From Cape Finisterre, Pytheas sailed east along the north of Spain to Corbilo on the mouth of the Loire, past Ushant to Land's End (Belerium), where he landed. He sailed all round Britain, and attempted an estimate of its circumference, and indicated the position of Ireland. Long before this, as we have just seen, the Beaker people came across the North Sea, and settled on our East Coast; so even the prehistoric period had its great seamen and sea-faring traditions.

This discussion of the trade routes enables us to take up the question of the position of the Cassiterides (from the Greek word for tin, *cassiteros*), or the tin islands of the ancients: were they really islands? The Greeks and Romans obtained tin from Galicia, Cornwall, and possibly the Scillies, but the main supply was from Cornwall, and possibly it is the British Isles which were the Cassiterides.

Pytheas says tin was conveyed by the people of Belerium in wagons, at low tide from the mainland, to the island of Ictis, where it was purchased by merchants, carried to Gaul, and transported on packhorses to Marseilles, the overland journey taking thirty days. To start with there has been considerable doubt as to the locality of Ictis; some think it was St. Michael's Mount, others the Isle of Wight or Thanet. The tin must have been mined in Cornwall, and it would have meant a long overland journey to the two latter places.

We have seen there were good sailors, and the general weight of evidence inclines us to accept the view that the tin was shipped at St. Michael's Mount, close to where it was mined. The fact that the Veneti formed the confederation against Caesar points to a predominance based on trade, and they may have controlled the tin traffic, in which case Corbilo would have been a natural place for unshipment.

From Corbilo to Marseilles is approximately 500 miles, which means nearly seventeen miles a day for the pack-horses on the thirty days' journey. The tin was cast into ingots, of the shape of ankle bones, and two of these made up the load for a pack-horse.

Britain has always been rich in metals. Copper is found in Cornwall, Cardiganshire, Anglesey, Snowdonia, and in Ireland. Tin in Cornwall and on Dartmoor. Prehistoric man would have obtained his copper from boulders, or found lumps of ore on the hillside, and tin from the gravel beds of streams. Ireland was El Dorado of the Old World, and gold was found in the Wicklow Hills as late as 1795. It was shipped across to Carnarvonshire, or the mouth of the Mersey, and from there found its way down by way of Shrewsbury, Craven Arms, Wootton Bassett, Sarum, and a deeper and more navigable Avon to Christchurch, and so across to Cherbourg. Another route appears to have been from the Mersey, across the Peak District to Peterborough and the Wash, where it was shipped to Denmark and north Germany.

It is interesting to see how, by mapping the finds of bronze implements, and gold ornaments, trade routes are established. Sea-borne traffic is shown by the large number of hoards of bronze implements, found near the sea coast, and around the estuaries of navigable rivers.

Going right back to Neolithic days, we find that flints were mined at Grime's Graves (Grime means the devil) in Brandon and at Cissbury near Worthing, and apparently only roughly chipped there and then exported to be finished elsewhere. They must have been carried along the trackways to the hill forts. These old trackways have interesting names. The Ridgeway comes from Fenland along the Dunstable Downs to Berkshire, the White Horse, and the Marlborough Downs; there is the Harroway coming from Cornwall, and finding its way through Hampshire to the Thames estuary; and the Pilgrims' Way, along the southern slopes of the North Downs, was an old road long before men tramped its surface to Becket's shrine at Canterbury.

Here we must attempt to sum up what we have found out about the Bronze Age. The introduction of metal opened up new activities for man, and especially new opportunities for the individual. The Neolithic man toiled with antler pick and shoulder-blade shovel, and piled earth in the banked camps. He chipped sarsen stones, and fidgeted them into the upright position of menhirs and dolmens. It was patient team work in which everyone laboured for the community. He needs must move from camp to camp to find pasture for his flocks. In much the same way primitive peoples like the Tasmanians, Australian aborigines, and the Eskimo are fully occupied in hunting to live; they have not any leisure for fighting, or any possessions to fight for. When everything has to be carried about, the lighter you travel the better.

The earlier round-heads appear to have been powerful, and may have been a pleasant people; we have seen that they were buried side by side in the same barrows with the older stock of Neolithic long-heads, and this points to friendly conditions.

As metal became more plentiful, larger clearings were made in the forests, and man began to settle down. He could grow more crops and keep more cattle; he began to have possessions. This was the opportunity for the individual; if a man was harder working than his fellows or more far-seeing, cleverer or more frugal, he could become a man of property, and, founding a family, become the chieftain. The tribe was gradually forged into a nation, and the chieftain became a petty king. With these added riches and possessions and the temptations they brought, we find the first traces of really warlike weapons, and it is probable that the Bronze Age saw the beginning of organized warfare.

We may be sure that this wider life brought in its train a set of problems which had not confronted the Neolithic herdsmen. As man began to have more possessions, he became alarmed for the safety of his own, or envious of those of others.

These people give proof of being able to work together, and so may have attempted, in a gradual way, to solve the problem of the right mode of living. Without some code or tradition, the community would have degenerated into a rabble. We shall find as we go along that man is tremendously concerned with this, and seeks many ways for his own government. We shall not be far wrong if we picture the Bronze Age people as living, like the Homeric Greeks, under kings and nobles, yet given some share in the framing of the law.

THE EARLY IRON AGE

HERE WE must start by another reminder: that at the
beginning of the Early Iron Age, which first saw the
introduction of that metal, men did not pack up all
their old bronze implements and bury them in hoards,
to at once arm themselves with iron. It was, on the
contrary, a very gradual change-over, and for a long
time both bronze and iron were used side by side. This
was so at Hallstatt in the Noric Alps of the Austrian
Tyrol. Here there have been salt mines from the
earliest times, and it must have been an important
trading centre. Excavations have been carried out in
the cemetery of the salt miners, and the implements
found there have been held to be distinctive of the
civilization at the beginning of the Early Iron Age,
when bronze was still in use.

The second half of the Early Iron Age is held to be
most typically shown by implements which have been
recovered from an old settlement, built on piles, on the
margin of a bay on Lake Neuchâtel, near Marin, to
which the name of La Tène, or the Shallows, has been
given. The finest developments of the Early Iron Age
are to be found in this country, since it fell under
Rome's influence at a later date than the Continent;
in the same way the Iron Age, or Late Celtic tradition,
survived in Ireland and parts of Scotland which were
never occupied by the Romans.

The people of England had become very mixed racially. On p. 24 we sketched the order of the arrivals of the different peoples; and just as bronze overlapped the use of iron, so the old peoples carried on their everyday life and were not always exterminated by the new-comers or even dispossessed of their lands. We saw how, in the early round barrows, the later round-heads were buried side by side with the earlier long-heads.

The next arrivals were the Goidels, or first of the Celtic-speaking peoples. On p. 28 we mentioned the generally accepted theory that they were driven into the west by their successors, the Brythons, who were related to them and spoke another variety of the Celtic language. This is now being given up, and it is thought that there were never any Goidels in England or Wales, but that they went directly to Ireland, the Isle of Man, and Scotland, where their Celtic descendants still live.

The Brythons were followed by the Marnian Celts who were responsible for the finest developments of what we now call Late Celtic art, and by the Belgae who were the latest of Britain's pre-Roman invaders. They came from where Belgium now is, and had more Nordic blood than their predecessors; they were a half-Teutonic and fierce fighting people.

We saw on p. 65 how the people of the Heathery Burn Cave were of long-headed stock, which yet had absorbed a Bronze civilization. Much the same thing occurs in the Iron Age at Glastonbury lake village, and we shall base our illustrations of the period on the houses and implements discovered there.

In Neolithic times the idea of building over water was developed, and in Switzerland there were dwellings built on the margins of lakes. They were first discovered at Ober-Meilen, Lake Zürich, in 1853, and this started research, and the discovery of similar structures in different parts of Europe. These may be divided into three types. (1) The Swiss dwellings, built on platforms formed on the tops of piles driven into the lake bed or more often into the marshy land at the edge of the lake, which date from the Neolithic and Bronze Ages. (2) Another type in which, instead of pile foundations, large open framings resembling log huts were sunk in the lake and steadied by piles, much like the modern caisson used by engineers for foundations. Dwellings of this type were built in France and Germany during the Early Iron Age. (3) The type like Glastonbury and the Scottish and Irish Crannogs. These were really small islands formed in the middle of marshes and, being stockaded around, were raised above the flood-level by earth brought from outside; but the foundation was quaking bog, which, as we shall see at Glastonbury, gave the inhabitants a great deal of trouble. These date from the Early Iron Age, and continued to be occupied in remote spots, as places of refuge, until the seventeenth century.

As the Swiss lakes became overpopulated, people moved downhill into the Po Valley, and here are found the settlements which are called Terremare, from *terra marna*, or marl earth. The peasants discovered that the earth from these old settlements was valuable for agricultural purposes, and in carting it away came across antiquities which disclosed the secret.

There are literary references to lake dwellings. Caesar said, writing of the Morini (a Belgic tribe in Gaul, opposite Kent): 'They had no place to which they might retreat, on account of the drying up of their marshes (which they had availed themselves of as a place of refuge the preceding year), and almost all fell into the power of Labienus' (*Com.* iv, c. 38).

Venice itself, the Queen of the Adriatic, is a glorified crannog which started as a place of refuge. 'They little thought, who first drove the stakes into the sand, and strewed the ocean reeds for their rest, that their children were to be the princes of that ocean, and their palaces its pride.'

Hereward the Wake maintained himself, in the last stand against the Normans, in the marshy recesses of the Isle of Ely.

Now we come to the interesting way by which we in England came to be provided with a lake village of our own. Mr. Arthur Bulleid of Glastonbury, when he was a young man, read Keller's *Swiss Lake Dwellings*, and was fired with the idea that there must have been a lake village in the olden days in the swamps near Glastonbury. Remember that in this neighbourhood there is the tradition of Arthur and his knights and the Isle of Avalon:

> 'The island valley of Avilion,
> Where falls not hail or rain, or any snow,
> Nor ever wind blows loudly.'

So whenever Mr. Bulleid went on his walks abroad he kept a wide-open eye for any indications of a possible site for a lake village. This was in the end discovered by the mounds which had been left where the hut foundations were, and though in the course of 2000 years or more the land had been drained, and became covered with vegetable soil and turf, yet these mounds were still noticeable to the observant eye. In the molehills were found pieces of bone and charcoal, and when Mr. Bulleid made a trial hole he came across

Fig. 53 Glastonbury lake village

more charcoal, some pottery, and two oak beams. Again, a labouring man, David Cox by name, told Mr. Bulleid that when he had been cleaning out a ditch about three-quarters of a mile away, in 1884, he had found a black oak beam embedded in the soil, and had to cut a piece off it to widen the ditch. Cox reported that this beam looked like the end of a boat, and this is what it turned out to be (Fig. 57). So Mr. Bulleid's dream had come true, and he had found his lake village. Excavations were started in 1892, since when the village has been thoroughly explored.

Fig. 53 gives a bird's eye view of the village. The area was about 10,530 square yards, and the foundations of the enclosed space were reinforced with layers of logs, laid down crossways, and filled in with brushwood, stones, and clay, but it could never have been what the land agents describe as a 'desirable building site'. During the time that Glastonbury was occupied, a bed of peat accumulated in some places 5 feet thick, and the inhabitants were constantly rebuilding. The village was palisaded around, with piles driven into the peat, and filled in with wattle and daub. This method was also used in the construction of the huts – there were 80 to 90 of these, roughly circular in shape, and varying from 18 feet to 28 feet in diameter; they may not all have been houses; some were probably used as barns or workshops. The huts contained a central hearth (Fig. 54) of flat stones let into a clay bed, and as many as nine or ten hearths have been found added one on the top of the other, as the foundations settled down into the bog. The wattled walls of the huts were daubed with clay; this is known because pieces of clay showing the marks of the wattles were discovered in the excavations. Each hut had a central pole or roof tree. We can gather little more than this.

Fig. 54 Hut interior at Glastonbury

We have to look to a primitive people, then, to find parallel building traditions. The Kikuyu, of Kenya, today build and live in houses which must be the same as those at Glastonbury. Fig. 55 shows these on the left-hand side of the section, and on the right is the suggested form of the Glastonbury hut. We have made this drawing from the plan and carefully detailed particulars in Mr. and Mrs. Routledge's book, *With a*

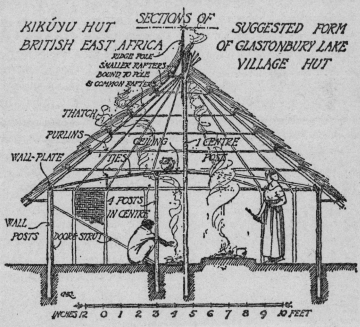

Fig. 55   Hut sections

Prehistoric People. It is an interesting fact that the constructional problem which the Kikuyu have to face, when they build their huts, is similar to the one which confronted Wren when he designed the dome of St. Paul's Cathedral.

Neolithic man sometimes built little houses with

rafters leaning against a central pole, and this was a very sound method. So long as the feet of the rafters were firmly fixed into the soil, the house stood firm, in gales and under a load of snow; the drawback was that there was no headroom around the walls, and so one had to sit there as in a bell-tent. A wall was raised around to give headroom, and this was satisfactory so long as the wall was built of stones heavy enough to provide a sufficient abutment for the thrust of the rafters. The trouble came when the same idea was attempted with thin wooden walls, which would have been overturned.

The Kikuyu first set up about nineteen forked posts in holes dug in a circle of about 15 feet diameter. To appreciate the cleverness of the construction, you must remember that none of the wood is thicker than a man's arm. Four posts are set up on an oblong in the centre about 4 feet 5 inches by 3 feet. Around the tops of the outer posts, long pliant rods are woven, and these form the wall plate, and take the thrust of the roof. Again ties are woven from this wall plate across from side to side, picking up the tops of the centre posts on the way. Wren took up the thrust of the brick cone which supports the dome and lantern at St. Paul's, by an iron ship's cable, which was let into the stone, and run in with molten lead. The rest of the construction of the Kikuyu hut is explained by the drawing.

At Glastonbury there were also found remains of an earlier type of hut, built with wall plates resting on the tops of piles driven into the peat. The huts were apparently oblong in shape, with hurdled walls mortised to the wall plates. Of these we cannot attempt any reconstruction, but of the circular huts we can be more sure, and it seems fair to assume, from what we know, that they resembled those of the Kikuyu.

This building in wattle and daub continued as a tradition throughout Celtic Britain. William of Malmesbury, writing in the twelfth century A.D., mentions

Fig. 56   Building a hut at Glastonbury

the 'Ealde Chirche', the ancient church of St. Mary of Glastonbury, built in the seventh century, of wattle-work.

We know that the Glastonbury people used canoes, for one was found by David Cox, to which reference has been made, and some form of canoe would have been absolutely necessary to the inhabitants of the village. Judged by the peat deposit, all this district around the River Brue must have been a vast morass in the olden days, and in times of flood an inland sea.

Fig. 57 Dug-out canoe and landing-stage at Glastonbury

The canoe (Fig. 57) is of the greatest interest – about 18 feet long, the flat bottom is 2 feet wide, 10 feet from the prow, and its maximum depth inside is 12 inches. It is becoming boat-like, and shows a notable development on Fig. 1, having a shapeable prow, and a graceful rise, or sheer, at bow and stern. The lake

Fig. 58 Rock engraving of two men fishing from a boat

villagers had a landing-stage and dock attached to their home, with vertical walls made of stout grooved oak planks driven into the peat, into which were fitted horizontal boards (Fig. 57). We know they went fishing, because lead net sinkers have been found. Their canoes would have been used to take them to their cornfields on the mainland; the island village had no room for these. A rock engraving drawn at the time shows two people fishing from a boat. You can see their fishing lines, and the boat has an anchor with a cross-piece and a heavy stone weight on the end, like some in use today. Many querns and millstones have been found; the earlier type (Fig. 14), and the later rotary types (Fig. 59). In these the lower stone was fixed, and had a wooden pivot in the centre. The top stone was fitted over this, and corn fed through the hole, made large enough to allow it, passed down, and was ground between the upper and lower millstones, coming out at the sides as flour. Small cakes were found at Glastonbury, made of unground wheat grains which had been mixed probably with honey and baked.

Fig 59   Grinding corn

The villagers also owned horses; many harness fittings have been found, bits, and the wheels of chariots. Whether the horses were transported to the mainland on rafts or stabled there we cannot be sure. In the summer they may have been pastured on the mainland, within the protection of a camp, and in the winter ferried across to the village to share the huts with the inhabitants. The people doubtless used their canoes to carry on trade with the surplus goods which they manufactured and wished to exchange for other commodities. The two iron currency bars found point to this (*see* p. 134).

When we pass to the life carried on within the village, we have proof of many and varied activities, but it will perhaps be well to start by a description of the iron working, which gives the period its name.

Fireclay crucibles have been found at Glastonbury, and funnels (*tuyère*) for conducting the blast into the furnace, but it is thought that the crucibles were used for melting copper and tin, to make bronze, as described on p. 61.

So far as iron working was concerned, it is probable that this was carried out as the present-day smelting operations of the Kikuyu of Kenya, which we have shown in Fig. 60. The iron ore is collected from surface workings in the form of an iron sand; this is washed to get rid of the clay and other substances, so that the iron grains are left. The furnace consists of a kidney-shaped hole in the ground lined with clay. The ore is placed in the pit of the furnace, and a charcoal fire started, then more ore and charcoal are added as needed. The blast is introduced at one end of the furnace, which is slightly lower than the middle, by means of a fireclay funnel (*tuyère*). In the funnel are introduced the wooden pipes of the bellows, which are in this way protected from the fire. Two bellows are

Fig. 60 Smelting iron

used, of goats' skins sewn into the shapes of rough cones, or fools' caps, the pipes being attached to the small ends. At the larger ends of the bellows, which are open, are fitted two short sticks, sewn to the skins, but leaving one-third of the circumference free. The smiths' boy holding the two sticks of the two bellows, two in each hand, opens first one bellow, as if the sticks were hinged at one end, and then the other, and closing the opening by shutting his hand, depresses the sticks, and kneads the ends of the bellows, sending forward a continuous blast into the furnace. This blast raises the temperature of the furnace, just as a fire is brightened up by ordinary bellows.

The ore is reduced to a sticky mass rather than molten metal; furnaces which will generate a sufficient heat to make the metal flow only date from the seventeenth century, and we do not find any cast iron before then. The lump of iron is left in the furnace overnight to cool, and then turned out in the morning, and broken up into sizeable pieces which are forged up into ingots or blooms. This iron is very pure, and ductile, and so can be readily forged; being smelted with charcoal it is free from the sulphur which comes from coal when it is used, and which makes the iron short and brittle. The fireclay crucibles we have referred to were buried in a hole in the ground, and the fire and blast arranged as in the case of the iron smelting.

In Messrs. Bulleid and Gray's book are shown illustrations of all the finds in the excavations, and here we can see daggers, spear-heads, swords, knives, bill-hooks, sickles, saws, gouges, adzes, files, bolts, nails, rivets, keys, and bits. The weapons are few and far between, and this is perhaps one of the reasons the

Fig. 61   Saw and adze

villagers fell an easy prey
to their enemies in the end.
The man in Fig. 54 is
holding an iron bill-hook
in his hand, of a quite
modern shape; and Fig. 61
shows one man using a
curiously shaped saw, with
the teeth arranged so that
it cuts on the upstroke,
while the other has an
adze, which is first cousin
to the axe. Fig. 62 shows a
man using a particularly beautiful iron knife found at
Glastonbury.

Fig. 62 An iron knife

Leaving iron working, we can turn to bronze, which
still continued in use in the Early Iron Age as it does
today.

Fig. 63 shows a penannular (almost a ring) brooch.
The top drawing shows how the pin,
which was loose on the ring, was
pushed through the material, and then
fastened by moving the ring round a
little, and clipping it under the pin.
This form of brooch was the forerunner
of the buckle.

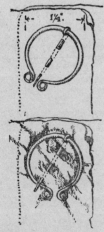

Fig. 63 Penann-
ular brooch

Fig. 64 shows three bronze brooches,
or *fibulae*. These fastenings came into
use in the Swiss and Italian lake villages
when cloth was first woven. The three
examples drawn here show the development of these pretty little things,
which the archaeologists associate
with the lake village of La Tène, on the
lake of Neuchâtel, and are called types

1, 2, and 3, though only type 2 occurs at La Tène itself. In 1 the foot is bent back until it touches the bow of the brooch. In 2 the end is no longer free but actually attached to the bow, and in 3 the foot and bow are designed as one.

On the right-hand side of Fig. 64 we have drawn the development of the springs of these brooches, and in each case the pin of the brooch is shown vertically. In those of Hallstatt the springs are on one side of the head; those of La Tène are bilateral: 1 shows the earliest type, like that of a safety-pin of today; 2 has a double coil; and in 3 the pin has one coil to the right, and the wire is then carried to the left, where, after a treble coil, it swings up to form the bow of the brooch. In 4 there is a double coil on both sides, and in 5 a treble coil, but the tension is increased by the ingenious way in which the loop or chord across is taken under the arch of the bow; the whole pin – coils, loop, and bow of the brooch – being in one unbroken length. In 6 we have pin and coils to the right, the loop or chord and the coils on the left in one piece; but the bow is a separate part which is hooked under the chord: 8 is on the same principle, but the spring is covered with a metal sheath attached to the bow. In 7 the bow is fixed on to a smaller loop. We consider these springs of the greatest importance: 1 dates from perhaps as early as 400 B.C., and 8 takes us up to the Roman occupation, and, so far as we know, 1 is the first application of the spring. The old brooch-maker who, in 400 B.C., tapped his bronze wire around a rod and discovered the spring, would have been rather surprised if he could have looked into the future and seen the many ways to which his invention would be applied; for example, that we should tell the time by little spring-driven machines, which we call watches.

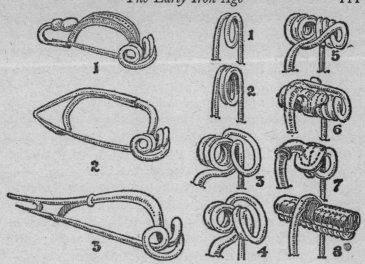

Fig. 64   Brooches and brooch springs

There were excellent potters at Glastonbury, and Fig. 54 shows some of the pottery found there. The greater part of it appears to have been hand-made, as described on p. 40, but the very beautiful pot in the foreground has been turned on some sort of wheel. We saw (p. 40) how the Kikuyu build up their pots on a pad of leaves, which makes it possible to turn the pot round as it is being made, and it is probable that the potter's wheel was preceded by a turn-table, on the lines of the rotary quern (Fig. 59). If a heavy block of stone or wood were pivoted in this way, its weight would aid the momentum of its spin and be very helpful in making pottery. This early type is suggested in Fig. 75(A)

Spinning and weaving were carried on in the village, and the spindle whorls and loom weights suggest that this work was done as already described on pp. 67–70.

There were expert coopers at Glastonbury, who knew how to build up tubs with wooden staves and hoops. They were good turners. There is a turned bowl, shown in the lower right-hand corner of Fig. 54, which was decorated in addition with a beautiful running pattern cut in an incised line. There is no evidence of what the Glastonbury lathe was like, but Fig. 65 shows a very primitive type in use in the Chilterns, called the pole lathe. It is difficult to see how anything could be simpler than this, and it is obviously a development from the bow-drill. In the Chilterns the men who make chair legs buy a fall of beech in the woods, and to save cartage build themselves little huts and turn the chair legs there. The supports for the lathe are often two trees growing close together, which they cut down at a height suitable for the two planks forming the bed of the lathe, into which the poppet heads are fixed. A third sapling is bent down, and the cord, which is to transmit the power, is fastened to this, passed around the chair leg, and connected to the treadle under. A rough tool-rest is provided. The turning is done on the down stroke, which revolves the chair leg towards the turner, and when he takes the pressure off the treadle, the pole pulls it up again ready for another cut. The work proceeds very rapidly, and we have seen chair legs turned as fast as one a minute.

In our sketch (p. 114) we have shown the turner making a wooden bowl, like the ones which were used before the days of enamelled iron. The block of wood was placed directly against one centre of the lathe, and on the other side came a circular piece of wood, around which the cord was passed; this was put on to the other centre of the lathe and fixed to the block for the bowl by four brads. This, we think, shows that the so-called

Kimmeridge coal-money is the core left from turning shale bracelets on pole lathes. Coal-money is found near the Kimmeridge shale beds on the Dorset coast, and consists of circular discs, having a hole on one side, and a square recess or two or three smaller holes on the other. The diagram at the bottom of Fig. 65 shows how we think a shale bracelet was turned on a pole lathe. AA are the poppet heads, and BB the centres, C is the circular piece of wood around which the cord was passed, fitted on to one centre, and let into one side of the piece of shale, in a square recess, or by two or three separate pins, the shale being in contact with the other centre. The turner trued up his bracelet, and set its outside shape first, and then making a cut on each face, finally detached it as dotted line D, and the Kimmeridge coal-money was the useless core, and never used as money. One great advantage of these old pole lathes was that the turner could make two or three bowls in graduating sizes from the same block of wood.

The Glastonbury carpenters used axes, and we do not realize in these days what a useful tool this can be – that is, to a craftsman and not a wood butcher. Alex. Beazeley, an architect, wrote in 1882 that the Swedish carpenters at Dalcarlia and Norrland, 'require no other tools than the axe and the auger, and despise the saw and plane as contemptible innovations, fit only for those unskilful in the handling of the nobler instruments: they will trim and square a log forty feet long as true as if it had been cut in the sawmill, and will dress it to a face that cannot be distinguished from planed work.' We shall find the truth of this – so long as man is master of his tools we get good work, but when the machine masters the man we have indifferent results.

Fig. 65 A pole lathe

The form of lake villages suggests that they were built by timorous people, living in fear of fiercer neighbours. They appear to have had their beginnings with the long-headed Mediterranean race of the New Stone Age. The Glastonbury lake villagers belonged to the Marnian Celtic stock who inhabited much of Britain at this time, and were famous for that highly decorated and enamelled woodwork. The Marnian Celts are believed to have come from the valley of the Marne river, north of Paris. A man of similar racial stock was found in a bog like those around Glastonbury in Denmark. The peat has preserved the body perfectly, as it preserved the Glastonbury houses – we can tell from the contents of his stomach what he had eaten, and his face provides us with the first prehistoric portrait from the life. These men were small and dark – 5 feet 3 inches to 5 feet 8 inches in height – oval-headed, with a cephalic index of 76, which makes them of mesaticephalic type. The same physical stock lived at Worlebury Camp, at the west end of the trackway on the Mendips, and in Romano-British times in the villages of Woodcuts, Rotherley, and Woodyates, in Cranborne Chase, down to Saxon times.

At Glastonbury their fears held true, and some little time before the Roman occupation final disaster descended on the village, and they were put to the sword: perhaps by the Belgic invaders, who were long-heads, but of an altogether tougher fighting breed. Caesar (*Com.* v, c. 43) tells us how the Nervii, when attacking Cicero's camp, set fire to the thatch of the huts, by discharging red-hot clay sling bullets. Many of these were found at Glastonbury, and help us to visualize the final scene. We have noted that very few arms were found in the excavations, and the little dark men only wanted to be left quietly alone, and be

allowed to get on with their work; and this is what they
did until they were discovered. Then their outlying
possessions and crops would have been destroyed, and
the village surrounded. The Glastonbury men could
only have watched the scene, in shuddering misery,
from behind their stockades, and then the invaders,
using perhaps the dug-outs they had collected from
the waterside, would have paddled across the lake, and
discharging their red-hot clay bullets have fired the
thatch. When the flames subsided, the few survivors
would have been put to the sword. Yet the little dark
men have had their revenge; from the very start of
their career they appear to have lived in communities;
it may have been a tradition they brought with them
from the shores of the Mediterranean. The Belgae who
oppressed them, like the later Anglo-Saxons, whom
they resembled, preferred a more open-air life, and
today their fair-haired descendants have the same
tastes.

Professor Fleure, in his paper on the *Racial History of
the British People*, sums up the matter thus: 'These
descendants of the Neolithic people are the long-
headed, long-faced, dark-haired, brown-eyed people
that form so strong an element of the population of big
English cities. They seem better able than all other
types to withstand slum conditions, so that in the
second generation of great city life they have arisen in
their millions to form once more, after many days,
almost a majority, perhaps, of the population of south
Britain.' So the tale of the Mediterranean men is not
yet completed.

Having seen something of men's houses in the Early
Iron Age and the more domestic details of their lives,
we can turn to their larger works. The trackways, or

road system, link up a series of splendid earthworks, and many of these are of Iron Age construction. Starting perhaps as simple cattle enclosures, surrounded by a ditch and bank, with some additional precautions, taken at the entrances, these camps were gradually improved, until we arrive at such a masterpiece as Maiden Castle near Dorchester. More banks were added, the entrances made into mazes of ingenuity, and the whole developed just in the same way as the Tower of London, where we find the Norman keep surrounded by much later works.

It is very difficult to estimate the age of earthworks, especially the very simple ones. In some, Roman coins have been found, but this would not justify us in saying that an earthwork was Roman. The Romans fortified their camps when on the march, but did not often occupy the Iron Age hill forts. Roman coins in these may point to the times of the Saxon terror, when the Britons fled to these forts as places of refuge and took their money with them.

Earthworks are classified by archaeologists as A, Promontory Fortresses, where a piece of high ground inaccessible by reason of precipices or water on one side, has been defended by artificial works on the other. B 1 are Hilltop Forts with artificial defences following the natural lines of the hill, and are sometimes called Contour Forts. B 2 are forts on high ground, less dependent on natural slopes for protection, and there are later types which do not concern us now.

It may be well to give first a brief description of the terms used in describing an earthwork. Vallum, rampart, and agger, all mean earthen walls. Fosse or ditch, an escarpment is the outer slope, while the counterscarp is the inner slope; if the counterscarp is brought up above the level line as a smaller rampart, this is a revetment. The flat piece of undisturbed ground between the ramparts is a berm. The plans of earthworks, which generally look like hairy caterpillars biting their tails, show the top of a slope as a thick line tapering off down the slope.

Now as to the way the builders went to work. To start with, they had as good an eye for the possibilities of a piece of country as a Royal Engineer officer, or a fox-hunting squire. They always chose pleasant sunny situations where the thyme-scented grass gave good feeding for their cattle, and the scabious flowers nodded in the breeze to the song of the skylark. There is no more pleasant place in which to loaf than an old earthwork; you can always get into the sun and out of the wind, and the slope of the banks is exactly right for an easy position from which to gaze over the countryside, and that is just what the old men wanted to do. Their cattle would have grazed on the hillside, meanwhile the watchman kept a look out for wolves and wild boar, or wandering cattle-lifters. Cattle were wealth in those days.

The builders then chose the rounded hump of a chalk down, which was not controlled by any higher ground, and it is probable that the first thing they did was to dig one simple ditch and bank, or fosse and vallum. They doubtless carried up the chalk in rough baskets, and so raised the bank above them. On examining an old earthwork, the first thing to do is to discover the natural level, and then see how they went to work, because at first sight the fosses are so deep, and the banks so high, that it seems impossible such work could have been done without steam navvies. When we have found the natural level we discover that the art of the job was that, by the basket of earth dug out, not only was the ditch lowered, but the bank raised, and that a higher bank was made more speedily on a slope than on the level. Again, on a very steep slope the soil dug out could be thrown downhill.

Still, notwithstanding all this, these earthworks must have been tremendous undertakings. The outermost of the three banks at Badbury, near Wimborne, Dorset, is one mile in circuit; at Maiden Castle, near Dorchester, nearly 1½ miles. Particular care was given to the design of the entrances. At Badbury there are two, one on the east and the other the west. On the west side the banks have been cut through in other places in recent times, but originally any invading force had to enter by these two ways, which left it very much at the mercy of the bowmen on the banks above them. A 'flanking' entrance was so arranged that the right side (unprotected by shield) was exposed to the defenders' arrows. The tops of the banks were palisaded, and the bottoms of the ditches were perhaps filled with sharpened stakes. The wide areas between the banks, called 'berms', may have been used as cattle pens – a stampede of half-wild cattle at night would not have been pleasant – or, as at Maiden Castle, the camp may have been divided into two parts for the same purpose.

Hut circles are found in the earthworks, which suggests huts as shown in our drawings. Heaps of sling stones have been found, and bracers, or wrist-guards, which show that bows were used.

There has been considerable discussion as to how the Hill Fort men provided themselves with water, and there are various theories. First, it must be remembered that the fort formed the citadel, and place of refuge for the district, and the people grouped themselves around it. Their little huts were not difficult to make, and their simple husbandry meant only the cultivation of the terraces, or lynchets, on the hillside where they grew their corn; they did not need or use so much water as we do today, and in the usual way were free to go downhill to the nearest stream. However, at Maiden Castle, excavation revealed an intricate system of tunnels and gutters on the chalk floor converging on certain pits. These pits may have been lined with sewn skins to make watertight cisterns and the gutters possibly puddled with clay so that these hill forts could be supplied with water in time of seige. Then there is the dew pond, which is still used to water cattle on the Wiltshire Downs. This is made as Fig. 66. A shallow saucerlike depression is cut in the chalk, and

Fig. 66   A dew pond

lined with straw. On this comes a layer of puddled clay, with rims of chalk to protect the clay from the feet of cattle. Loose flints are put on the bottom, and the pond is started with a little water in it. The straw and clay cut off the heat of the earth, and when the moist mists drive over the Downs at night and come to the cooler pond, they condense on its surface. Ordinary ponds are formed in this way, where a pocket of clay comes in a warmer soil. Water drains into it, and the cattle puddle up the clay till it is free from cracks and watertight, and so the pond extends.

In the hot summer of 1921 we were going through Dorset looking at earthworks, and found the pond on the top of Holt Heath, near Bull Barrow, full of water, while the Tarrant river in the valley close by was absolutely dry. The Wycombe chair-makers, who go into the woods to turn chair legs, obtain water in an ingenious way. If you examine the bole of a beech tree you will find well-marked channels where the rain and condensed dew runs down the tree-trunk. The chair-maker makes a cross cut in such a channel, and drives in a chip of wood which diverts the water into a pail; turning on a tap is not the only way to get water.

The concentration of a number of people either making or living in a hill fort was to have great results. In the old days, the hunting tribe was like a large family, who very speedily knew all one another's good points, and were so apt to emphasize the bad ones; life was not at all exciting. Here there must have been a bustling life, with all kinds of men coming and going, and new things to be discovered. Customs would arise, and Law solidify out of these. Language would develop around the hut fires, and traditional tales form the beginnings of literature. These hill forts are evidences of a more ordered system of life than anything which had gone before; even today with our transport system, and organized labour, the construction of either Bad-bury or Maiden Castle would call for concentrated effort. To make a flint or metal implement, which you do yourself, is one thing; to construct a camp which needs the labour of many men is quite another. It had to be planned; there must have been some few men who were skilled in the design of camps, and could say to the tribesmen, 'Today we will cut this ditch, and dump the stuff here to form a bank. You are going wrong there; and you have not allowed sufficient room for that escarpment, because the angle of repose at which chalk will come to rest is flatter than that', and so on.

If our readers read Mr. Hippisley Cox's book, *The Green Roads of England*, they will find how these hill forts are all linked up on a trackway system, as well adapted to the needs of the time as the Roman roads and stations later on. This road question brings up fortification, and what it means. Let us imagine Badbury, not grass grown as it is today but all shining white where the chalk banks had been thrown up; or Maiden Castle, 1½ miles round its outer circuit. It must have been startlingly formidable in appearance. As the later tribes came in as immigrants, and found their way along the trackways, these hill forts were there to bar their way. Of course, there were not any invading armies in those days, who needed to maintain lines of communication with the coast; the invaders were tribes who wished to settle down. In the case of hostile tribes, they certainly could not afford to cross a trackway and leave a hill fort on their flank or rear, unless they came to terms with its inhabitants. In this way these hill forts played exactly the same part as the Norman Castles and walled towns of the Middle Ages.

We have seen how fond the ancient Britons were of wattlework, and on p. 103 how it was used even for the construction of churches. Boats were made in this way, and Fig. 67 shows a coracle, of which the wattled framework was covered with hide; coracles are still in occasional use by fishermen on Welsh rivers. Primitive peoples frequently make boats in this way. Fig. 68 shows the framework of the umiak, or women's boat of the Eskimo, made of driftwood, laced together with thongs, without a single nail, and covered with skins; and Fig. 69 how it is fitted with a mast, and square sail of membrane. Later Bronze Age or Iron Age rock

Fig. 67 Coracles

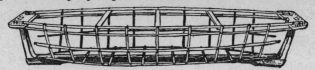

Fig. 68   Framework of umiak

engravings from Europe show a heavy sea-going vessel like a Viking Long Ship, with a high curved stern and an animal totem at the prow. Everyone in these boats seems to be rowing furiously (Fig. 70). Fig. 71 shows swords of the Early Iron Age: 1 shows an early Halstatt pattern, and 2 a later La Tène type shown in scabbard. The scabbards were in bronze, and frequently orna- mented with very beautiful designs. The sword blade was of iron, with a tang on to which was fitted a bronze mount to the handle, the latter formed of bone or wood threaded on to the tang.

Fig. 71 also shows two iron spear-heads of the same

Fig. 69   Eskimo umiak

period which are
rather different
from the leaf-
shaped patterns
of the Bronze
Age. The shields
were now oblong
in shape. This
spendid work of
art can be seen
at the British
Museum, and is
made of bronze
decorated with

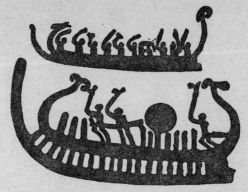

Fig. 70   Rock engraving of two Bronze or Iron Age war vessels

enamels. This form of decoration appears to have developed out of the use of coral, added as an ornament
to bronze. Then Early Iron Age metalworkers made
studs, with an enamel surface, and pinned these to the
bronze. This led the way to the crowning glory of

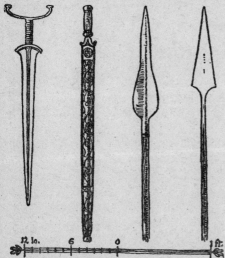

Fig. 71   Early Iron Age swords and spears

their work, Cham-
plevé enamelling.
Here the field of the
design was graved
out of the metal,
and the ground be-
ing first scored to
give a key was filled
in with the fused
enamel, which,
being polished, was
finished flush with
the face. Fig. 72, of
an enamelled har-
ness ornament,
shows to what

Fig. 72   Enamelled harness ornament

mastery of line the designers had now advanced. Think of the splendid appearance of an Early Iron Age chieftain; his helmet, shield, and horse-mountings all bronze, not dull as now but shining like gold, with the enamels afire like liquid rubies. The earliest enamels were of one colour, red.

In the Early Iron Age, costume had developed and weaving in brilliant colours was practised. It is thought that these were combined into primitive tar-

Fig. 73   Two Scythian men wearing trousers, drawn
on an Iron Age vessel

tans. As in the Bronze Age, a piece of material was folded around the body, in the form of a kilt, and this with a sleeveless vest, and a cloak which was semi-circular in shape, completed a man's attire. The shoes were cut out of hide, with straps attached, and gathered round the ankle. The Brythons appear to have introduced the loose trousers, which originated with the Persians and Scythians (Fig. 73). The women wore a long tunic reaching to the ankles, with short sleeves. Women, men, and horses, all alike, wore beautiful torcs, belts, and brooches, of bronze and enamel.

Another thing which was not found at Glastonbury was the burial-place, so that we do not know what objects they buried with their dead; fortunately for archaeologists, there are many other Early Iron Age cemeteries also belonging to the Marnian Celts where this information can be gained. A very important one is at Arras, near Market Weighton, in the East Riding of Yorkshire; here the barrows are small, circular in form, not more than 2 feet high by about 8 feet diameter. The body was not cremated but buried in a very contracted position in a cist, or grave cut in the chalk. The skulls show the people to have been long-headed (*dolichocephalic*), and here for the first time iron is found with the body. This means either that there had been a reversion to the old burial customs of the Neolithic people, or that these were introduced afresh from the Continent; in any case the cremation of the Bronze Age passes away. Again, the long-headed skulls may point to a survival of Neolithic people, who had absorbed the old round-headed Bronze Age invaders, or to fresh invasions from the Continent. Some of the barrows at Arras and elsewhere in Yorkshire, were found to contain the remains of chariots, and these resemble the chariot burials in France; this rather points to the Yorkshire barrows being the work of invaders. The tyres of the chariots there are about 2 feet 8 inches in diameter, and parts of the oak rims or fellies were found, mortised for as many as sixteen spokes. There were nave collars, for the hubs, of iron plated with bronze, and the skeletons of horses of about thirteen hands. We saw the beginnings of chariots at

Heathery Burn Cave in the Bronze Age, and it is obvious that by the time of the Early Iron Age these played an important part in everyday life. Many of the Yorkshire barrows suggest that women were buried in them. In one were found one hundred glass beads of a beautiful deep blue colour, ringed and spotted with white; others were of clear green glass with a white line. There were rings of amber and gold, and bracelets of bronze. In the mounds were broken pottery, and the bones of animals, and charcoal, as if there had been a funeral feast. An iron mirror was found at Arras, very much rusted of course. Fig. 74 shows one of bronze of a more usual type.

Fig. 74   The Bronze mirror

Fig. 76 shows late Celtic ornament. We saw by Fig. 47 how the Bronze Age people's patterns were chevrons, lozenges, and concentric circles, and the Early Iron Age saw the introduction of the curve, and the endless possibilities which come about through combinations of curves.

We can now pass on to the latest type of burials in this country, and there is but little doubt that these were the work of Belgic invaders. They were discovered in 1886, at Aylesford in Kent. This was in the Belgic country, and here we find that cremation had again been introduced, and the Belgae appear to have maintained this custom.

The cist, or grave, covered by a barrow, had passed out of fashion, and its place had been taken by a circu-

Fig. 75 A potter's wheel

lar pit, about 3 feet 6 inches deep, the sides and bottom of which were daubed with chalky clay. In the pit were found burnt bones, and the fragments of the pottery cinerary urns, in which there had been placed a pail, flagon, skillet, or shallow saucepan, and brooches all of bronze. The custom evidently still persisted of burying objects which had belonged to the dead, because it had some symbolical meaning; or for their use in the spirit world; or because it would have been unlucky to retain the objects in everyday use. The flagon of a very beautiful shape must have been imported from Italy.

The Aylesford pottery marks a great advance. It is of very graceful shape, and must have been turned on a wheel, and given a lustrous black surface in the firing. The wheel may have been of the turn-table type described on p. 111, and shown at A in Fig. 75, or the potters may have advanced as far as the wheel shown at B. This is a very primitive type, which was used until lately for making flower-pots and bread-pans.

Except for this important detail of the reintroduction of cremation, the Belgae do not seem to have effected any very great alteration in the everyday life of the times. They were a fierce fighting people, and conquered the south-eastern districts. This gave them possession of the iron mines of the Sussex Weald, which

Fig. 76   Celtic patterns

was to be the Black Country of England until the eighteenth century.

The Brythons and the older Goidelic stock of the Bronze Age, and the Marnian Celts at Glastonbury and Arras, learned to use iron but continued to live their lives in their own way.

There are still a great many things which remain a puzzle to the archaeologist about the everyday doings of all those people who lived here before the coming of the Romans, when our written story began. Prominent among them is how they managed for communications and transport. It was seen (p. 51) how the stones forming the inner ring at Stonehenge, each weighing many tons, were brought all the way from Prescelly Mountains on the Pembrokeshire coast. This, as the crow flies, is about 150 miles. How could such a feat of transportation have been accomplished in 2000 B.C.? Either they were brought by land, making a wide détour to avoid the Severn Estuary, when thick virgin forest and wide marshes covered so much of the lower ground, or they must have come by sea, starting in the open Atlantic, weathering the rocky promontory of Cornwall, and beating up the chops of the English Channel. Yet we know nothing of their ships and very little of their roads, though a few of the many ancient trackways on the higher ground show some evidence of having been in use as early as the time of the Bronze Age population. And why bring those great stones at all? Were they moved in slow stages as holy indispensables in a tribal migration as the Ark of the Covenant was carried by the Israelites in the Bible? Or was it a mystical act of conquest such as prompted Edward the First to take the Stone of Scone from Scotland to London? Or was it that Prescelly Top was regarded as more sacred than Salisbury Plain and the transfer of its rock regarded as sanctifying the great shrine – just as we sometimes have water from the Jordan brought over here for christenings.

The tracks which run along the crests of the chalk downlands and the Cotswold Hills all go over ground which has been less disturbed by the building and agricultural operations which have altered the face of this densely populated country during the Middle Ages and the more strenuous later times. For that reason they were used by the cattle-drovers right down to the end of the last century. So they have been well preserved and are well marked.

But the Bronze Age people were scattered all over the country and the uniform evenness of their culture indicates that they must have had a fair system of communications, if only by bridle-paths. Recent archaeological research in Sussex has revealed the presence of Bronze Age farms, and one observes that the roadways leading to these were fair-sized tracks and not mere bridle-paths.

As to the Iron Age, it is most likely that there were paved roads. A settlement was excavated in Anglesey where a road of this kind and apparently of ancient date went right through its midst. And not far from the same place, in 1942, a most remarkable find was made of a quantity of iron tyres belonging to chariot-wheels. But if there were roads, even indifferent ones, there remains the problem as to who maintained them. That means a higher order of civilization than we usually credit our prehistoric ancestors with. Still, we must remember that the Bronze Age seems to have had more than a thousand years of peace, and if the tribes of the Iron Age were sufficiently well organized to make such vast earthworks as at Maiden Castle and Old Oswestry they may have maintained some sort of roads in the pauses between intertribal hostilities. Besides, in many things they imitated the Romans who were making such a stir with their conquests and their new way of things on the Continent. So that when the Caesars arrived they had little difficulty in attracting the populations of the hillforts into Romanized tribal centres.

Camulodunum, or Colchester, was the chief town of the Trinovantes; Verulamium, or St. Albans, of the Catuvellauni, and Cassivellaunus was their king. Caesar is supposed to have referred to St. Albans, when he wrote of 'an oppidum with the Britons is a place amidst dense forest, fortified by a rampart or ditch, whither it is their habit to assemble to escape an enemy's raid'. Corinium (Cirencester) was the home of the Dobuni; Calleva (Silchester) of the Atrebates; London of the Cantii. Women were allowed to be Queens. Cartismandua was Queen of the Brigantes, and their country was the Pennines, and Boudicca (Boadicea) Queen of the Iceni.

In the Bronze Age chapter we discussed trade and traffic (p. 89); and this brings up the question of money or the currency which is used as a medium for that exchange of goods which is the basis of Trade. It has been suggested that the gold bracelets of the Bronze Age may have been used as money; these have been found with rings fastened to them, and are called ring-money, and the idea does not seem too wildly remote. This is hardly the case with Fig. 77, which illustrates iron currency bars, and we can imagine our readers, unless they are born financiers, saying 'How on earth could anyone buy anything with a kind of iron walking stick'. We are quite sure that

Fig. 77   Currency bars

many have been puzzled by the various methods which have been adopted by different peoples. There was the British sovereign of gold, now unhappily not in general use; its dirty greasy successor, so typical of the time, the Treasury note; one has heard of cowrie-shells, and so on; in all parts of the world different things seem to be used, but none so odd perhaps as the iron bars of the Early Iron Age.

Of the two currency bars found at Glastonbury, one is $27\frac{7}{8}$ inches long, and weighs 4666 grains, the other, $21\frac{1}{4}$ inches, but much thicker than number one, weighs 9097 grains. Mr. Reginald Smith has identified currency bars with the *taleae ferreae* of Caesar (*De Bello Gallico* v, 12), and it is thought that there were six varieties, the British unit being about 4770 grains. Bars of $\frac{1}{4}$, $\frac{1}{6}$, 1, $1\frac{1}{2}$, 2 and 4 units have been identified.

Perhaps we can give an illustration which will show how these things become accepted as currency. In remote villages in this country not long ago, it was usual to have a settling-up day once a year after harvest; during the rest of the year the people ran bills, which they chalked up on the barn door. At settling time the farmer would go to the miller and say, 'How do we stand', to which the miller replied, 'I have ground your corn, and you had some of the flour, but I sold the remainder, and owe you £5'. The miller went to the baker who said, 'Yes, I had my flour from you, but supplied you with bread, and owe you £5'. The butcher bought his beasts from the farmer, but sold his meat to all the village, and so they weighed up the matter, and came to a settlement. It is quite conceivable that the same £5 note, with a little small change, would have passed from hand to hand, and enabled the village to start on another year's trading all square; if instead of the £5 note, you had an iron bar, it really did not matter so much – in fact it was rather better, because like our extinct gold sovereign, it was a thing of value itself, which is more than can be said of the Treasury note. Intertribal and international trade, though more complicated, was, and still is, conducted on this same basis, of the exchange of commodities. It is well to remember this, when so large a part of what is called business today is in reality only a gamble with the product of other men's labour. Real wealth springs from mother earth, and real work is to be engaged in winning or shaping her treasures.

We find a less extraordinary currency than the iron bars, about 150 to 200 B.C., in a British gold coinage of modern type of two values. This appears to have started in the south-east and as some of these coins are inscribed, it shows that writing had progressed.

The unit system of the currency bars is proof of some system of weights and measures, and another is given by the beautiful pots, bowls, and metal work. A good craftsman does not make a thing to just any odd size. Use will have shown him what is the handiest weight, and the best size. A modern brick, for example, is of the size and weight that experience has shown the bricklayer can handle. Endless experiment has gone to prove this, and all the other details of everyday work and the tallies or the sticks, which were kept as a reminder, became in time recognized standards and measurements.

The currency bars are proof of the exchange of commodities, but do not help us to understand how values were fixed; how much corn a plough was worth. With such necessaries of life, the plough was worth the extra amount of corn the farmer could grow by its use; that would be its just price in theory. In practice it is often regulated by scarcity, which tends to increase the price of the plough, or by overproduction, when the price of ploughs goes down. Then there are luxuries, for which people will pay more than they are worth, because they are beautiful, or very scarce, and so on. All this wants to be borne in mind; we shall find how in the Middle Ages, Canon Law was very much concerned with the Just Price and Usury, and even today a profiteer is not held to be a very pleasant person. Trade and currency bars; weights and measures; the honesty of the good man, and even the thieving of the rogue, are part of that wonderful peep-show into the past we call History, and cannot be neglected.

Now as we are approaching the end of our space, it may be as well to see if we can discover anything of the animating spirit which inspired these people, and gave savour to their everyday life. In Neolithic times men are thought to have worshipped the powers of Nature, with a great Mother God over all. Gildas, a monk, writing in the sixth century A.D., said: 'Nor will I cry out upon the mountains, fountains, or hills, or upon the rivers, which now are subservient to the use of men, but once were an abomination and destruction to them, and to which the blind people paid divine honour.' Yet Nature worship still lingers with stones which are lucky, and wells whose waters are curative.

Sun worship appears to have been typical of the early Bronze Age, and with the arrival of the Celts may have taken the form of hero worship. It is probable that in the Early Iron Age, as the gods became more personal and intimate, they took to themselves as well the failings of man; as they were stronger and braver than man, in the perpetual warfare they waged with the powers of darkness, so also they were more cruel and hard.

Druidism appears to have been the religion of the later Celtic tribes of Britain and Gaul, but doubtless it was grafted on to the Hero and Sun worship of the Bronze Age, and the older Nature and Moon worship of the Neolithic man. This has been a very general practice; a conquering people would be willing to place the credit of the victory to the power of their own gods, yet unwilling to neglect the ones who had been overthrown. A god was a god, even when associated with defeat, and might easily revenge himself by alliance with the powers of Darkness. It was wiser then not to run any risks, so we find old faiths adapted to new religions.

Caesar in *De Bello Gallico*, book vi, gives us an interesting picture of Druids and Druidism, and other sources of inspiration are the Celtic Myths and Legends that Mr. Squire has gathered together in his book. These tales have come down to us, because they were gathered together by monkish chronicles, from the twelfth to the fifteenth centuries, but for all the time before that they had been traditional in the Celtic countries, since the days when they were first recited by Druidical bards to the accompaniment of harps.

Caesar wrote of the Druids: 'As one of their leading dogmas, they inculcate this: that souls are not annihilated, but pass after death from one body to another,

and they hold that by this teaching men are much
encouraged to valour, through disregarding the fear of
death. They also discuss and impart to the young many
things concerning the heavenly bodies and their
movements, the size of the world and our earth,
natural science, and of the influence and power of the
immortal gods.' Again quoting Caesar: 'The whole
Gaulish nation is to a great degree devoted to super-
stitious rites; and on this account those who are
afflicted with severe diseases, or who are engaged in
battles and dangers, either sacrifice human beings for
victims, or vow that they will immolate themselves,
these employ the Druids as ministers for such sacrifices,
because they think that, unless the life of man be re-
paid for the life of man, the will of the immortal gods
cannot be appeased. Others make wicker-work images
of vast size, the limbs of which they fill with living men
and set on fire.'

From the little that is known, it can be gathered that
the Druids formed a religious aristocracy, to which
entrance could only be gained by a long novitiate.
There was a Head, or Pope, elected for life; they were
exempt from war and taxation; acted as judges, and
had a monopoly of learning. Time was reckoned by
nights, and the year counted by the revolutions of the
moon. White bulls were sacrificed before the mistletoe
was cut from the sacred oak. Captives were killed, and
signs read from the flow of their blood, and the palpi-
tation of their entrails.

The Gaulish Druids looked to their British brethren,
as possessed of a purer faith, and novices were sent
here to learn the mysteries. This came about because
the Continent fell under the influence of Rome at an
earlier date than we did; for the same reason, with the
advent of the Romans here, Druidism was driven into

the West, because its practices shocked even the Romans, until they finally routed it out of its headquarters in Anglesey. It survived in Ireland, which never fell under the Roman influence, until St. Patrick overthrew Cromm Cruaich.

If the Celtic legends are poisoned by hints of awful cruelty, we must yet remember that it was not the cruelty of the Romans, who enjoyed the killing in the Amphitheatre, but the religion of sacrifice carried to its most awful conclusion. The Druids were not cruel for cruelty's sake, but to propitiate the gods.

On the other side of the picture, we have the pleasant fact that the Celtic myths and legends, becoming traditional, were handed down, and became in the hands of the monkish chroniclers the foundation on which has been built a literature that is entirely our own.

We have seen what great artists the Celts were, when they turned to handicraft; their metal work, and enamels, have been the inspiration of many an artistic revival, hailed as new, and yet in reality just as old as the Druids.

The great Celtic festivals were Beltane at the beginning of May, Midsummer Day, the Feast of Lugh in August, and Samhain. We still have survivals of these in May Day, St. John's Day, Lammas, and Hallowe'en or All Saints, and the bonfires around which we dance on joyful occasions started life as the sacrificial pyres on which victims were burned to propitiate the gods, or cattle offered to stay the ravages of a murrain, or plague, at the original Celtic festivals.

INDEX

The numerals in heavy type denote the figure numbers of the illustrations